Earthbound

Sabine Helling

Ann Arbor
THE UNIVERSITY OF MICHIGAN PRESS

Copyright © by the University of Michigan Press 1997
All rights reserved
ISBN 0-472-08375-9
Library of Congress Catalog Card No. 96-61087
Published in the United States of America by
The University of Michigan Press
Manufactured in the United States of America

2000   1999   1998   1997   4 3 2 1

No part of this publication may be reproduced, stored in a retrieval system, or transmitted in any form or by any means, electronic, mechanical, or otherwise without the written permission of the publisher.

David Krise

Earthbound

Series Introduction

Content-based instruction (CBI) is the integration of content and language learning. **Alliance: The Michigan State University Textbook Series of Theme-based Content Instruction for ESL/EFL** is designed principally for postsecondary programs in English as a second/foreign language, though some books are appropriate for secondary programs as well. **Alliance** is the first series to allow programs to experiment with content-based language instruction (CBI) without the demands of teachers' time and effort in developing materials. It also offers a wide selection of topics from which both teachers and students can choose.

The rationale for a content-based approach to language instruction comes from the claim that interesting and relevant material increases motivation and promotes effective language learning. CBI also adheres to the pedagogical principle that teaching should build on the previous subject matter *and* second language knowledge of the learner, while taking into account the eventual uses the learners will make of the second or foreign language. Finally, with a content-based approach, students will grow in not one but three areas: second language acquisition, content knowledge, and cognitive development.

Three models of CBI at the postsecondary levels exist: theme-based, sheltered, and adjunct. The **Alliance** series utilizes a theme-based approach in which language skills, grammar, vocabulary, and cognitive skills are integrated into the study of one particular subject area. This model is advantageous in that it can be implemented in any postsecondary program and can be taught at all proficiency levels. Sheltered and adjunct courses, on the other hand, are limited to university settings with high-intermediate to advanced level students. The theme-based approach is also preferable for this series as it is the only approach that has as its principal goal the improvement of language competence rather than mastery of subject material.

Unique Features of the Series

All the textbooks have been piloted in the classroom by teachers other than the author. Because content-based instruction is a relatively new area of language teaching, our goal is to produce textbooks that are accessible to those teachers who have a great deal of experience with CBI and to those who have little or no experience. By piloting the textbooks with different teachers, we confirmed that people unfamiliar with the topic were able to teach the material easily. One teacher who taught one of the texts said, "I was hesitant at first because it has been many years since I studied this subject myself, but my fears were unfounded." This piloting also allowed the author to receive feedback on which activities worked and which didn't work, to determine whether or not the material was appropriate for the level and to check for any "loopholes" in the textbook.

The teacher's manual provides detailed explanations for those who may want more guidance for teaching the course. Detailed explanations and information for teaching the materials are in the teacher's manuals. Teachers can use or not use the information, depending on their experience, needs, and desires.

Each chapter in the student books states the content objectives, while teachers are provided with both content and language objectives in the teacher's manual. We expect that there is a range in teachers' philosophy toward CBI. Some teachers may accept wholly the idea that there should be no overt instruction of language and that students will naturally acquire the language through the content. Some, however, may feel that overt language instruction is necessary. By restricting the language objectives to the teacher's manual, teachers have the option to share them with their students or to use them only as information to guide their teaching. The omission of the language objectives from the student's book also allows teachers to further develop any material and not feel obligated to cover "specified" language objectives.

Explanations of language items are clearly shown in "language boxes." Important language points are explained in detail in "language boxes." These boxes give teachers the option to cover the material in class or to leave the information as reference for students to use on their own, depending on their philosophy toward CBI. The information in the language boxes also saves valuable time since teachers do not have to find the supporting language explanations from other textbooks.

Each book is devoted entirely to one particular content that builds on the students' previous learning experiences. This type of in-depth coverage allows topic-related vocabulary and concepts to be continuously recycled, thus increasing the students' knowledge of the content and language. Students will benefit from the coherence provided by an integrated skills approach with one unifying topical content.

The interests and needs of the learners are considered in the choice of topics. Our experience has shown that students have a wide variety of interests, some enjoying courses that are "entertainment" focused, such as music or film, while others prefer a more "academic" focus, such as American government or media. We have developed books that present different choices and are immediately relevant to and usable in students' lives.

Several choices of topics exist for beginner, intermediate, and advanced levels. As the student population varies from term to term, so will their needs and interests. Having more than one book to choose from at each level lets students choose the topics of special interest to them. Teachers can also choose topics they are comfortable with or interested in teaching.

Authentic materials are used whenever possible. One of the goals of CBI is to use original text that was created for a purpose other than language teaching. The structure, function, and discourse features in these materials then dictate what language is to be taught. While much of the information was kept in its original form, some of the authentic texts were adapted to match the language ability of the audience.

Content material is supplemented with activities that assist students in comprehension. The material in each book has been carefully analyzed to determine those language skills that will assist the students in comprehending the information. Activities have then been developed and any necessary language explanations to accomplish this goal have been included.

Language items are presented in an inductive format. This format encourages students to generate for themselves how or why a particular form is used. This "active" discovery helps students retain the information more successfully.

Format of the Books

Each book in the **Alliance** series follows the same format, except in the Vocabulary Development section, which is present in some books but not in others. This format is as follows:

Opening Activity: Each chapter opens with some sort of activity that will get the students thinking about the topic of the chapter. This opening activity may be as simple as a picture or may involve a detailed activity. Its purpose is not to master the content described but simply to raise the students' awareness of the topic.

A Look Behind/A Look Ahead: This section contains a brief review of the previous chapter and an overview of what the students will study in the current chapter.

To the Student: Each chapter lists the content objectives, and students are encouraged to read these before studying the chapter as a preview. They should also go over the objectives again at the end of the chapter to check for comprehension.

Vocabulary Development: Some of the texts include a section on vocabulary development so that the students have a list of the important chapter vocabulary words and can learn various strategies for developing that vocabulary.

Content Headings: The chapter is then divided into content areas marked with roman numerals. Within that content area, activities (labeled A, B, C, etc.) help students comprehend the material.

Series Acknowledgments

There are many people we need to thank for their help in making this series a reality. Most important, the authors deserve our gratitude for their dedication, insight, and cooperation toward the project despite their busy professional demands. We are also indebted to the entire staff at the English Language Center of Michigan State University. Whether or not they were directly involved, everyone was willing to adjust schedules to accommodate and support the needs of the project. From our original meeting, Mary Erwin, our project editor at the University of Michigan Press, has been our major supporter, urging, pushing, and cajoling us to meet deadlines. Her belief in this project has ultimately allowed these materials to see the light of day. In addition, we would like to thank Chris Milton along with the entire staff at the University of Michigan Press for working so hard to produce high-quality manuscripts in such a quick turnaround time. Special thanks also goes to Peter Shaw of the Monterey Institute, who initially envisioned this project.

We are aware that there are still many theoretical and practical issues left to be resolved surrounding content-based instruction. We hope the **Alliance** series will make some inroads toward the resolution of some of the issues and lead to a better acceptance of this approach to language teaching in the field of ESL/EFL.

Susan Gass—Project Coordinator
Amy Tickle—Series Editor

Author Acknowledgments

There are several individuals whom I would like to acknowledge for their contribution to this book. Most importantly, I would like to thank the series editor, Amy Tickle, for her helpful suggestions and revisions throughout the writing process. A crucial contribution to this book came from the art work by Luciano Picanco who took the time and patience to draw what, I thought, I had in my head. Two teachers, Ildiko Svetics and Gary Cook, piloted the course and contributed their valuable comments. Carol Lauderdale and, of course, the anonymous reviewers carefully read the manuscript and made suggestions at the beginning stages of the project. I would also like to thank Dr. Susan Gass, the director of the English Language Center (ELC), for her support in completing this project. The staff at the ELC deserves a "thank you" for creating a supportive working environment. Finally I would like to thank my husband and all my friends, especially Claudia Walters, for their feedback and support.

Sabine Helling

Acknowledgments

Grateful acknowledgment is made to the following publishers, newspapers, magazines, and authors for permission to reprint copyrighted materials:

©AAA for the map of Michigan. Reproduced by permission.

American Petroleum Institute for slides showing plate tectonics.

Ameritech for material from the 1996 Lansing Phone Book.

Associated Press for "China Shaken by Second Earthquake in Two Weeks!" in the *State News* 1/11/95. © 1995 Associated Press. Reprinted by permission.

Bildarchiv Preußischer Kulturbesitz for photograph of painting of Alexander von Humboldt by Friedrich Georg Weitsch.

Council of Foreign Relations, Inc., for material from an article which originally appeared in *Foreign Affairs* called "Ecological Roulette: Damming the Yangtze" by Audrey R. Topping, (Sept/Oct 95). Copyright 1995 by the Council on Foreign Relations, Inc.

Fulcrum Publishing for material from *Keepers of the Earth: Native American Stories and Environmental Activities for Children* © 1988 by Michael J. Caduto and Joseph Bruchac. With permission of the publisher, Golden, Colorado 80401 (800) 992-2908.

GeoSystems for the "World Time Zone Map" © R. R. Donnelley & Sons Co., 1993.

Glencoe/McGraw Hill for material from *World Geography*. Mission Hills, CA, 1989.

©Hammond Incorporated for maps of Ohio and Pennsylvania from *Discovering Maps: A Young Person's World Atlas*. Maplewood, New Jersey, 1991, license #12,275.

Harvard University Press for material reprinted by permission of the publishers and the Trustees of Amherst College from *The Poems of Emily Dickinson*, Thomas N. Johnson, ed., Cambridge, Mass. Copyright © 1951, 1955, 1979, 1983 by the President and Fellows of Harvard College.

Houghton Mifflin Company for material adapted and reproduced from *The American Heritage Dictionary of the English Language, Third Edition*. Copyright © 1996 by Houghton Mifflin Company.

Lansing State Journal for material from page 6B, Sunday, June 6, 1993.

Larousse Kingfisher Chambers Inc., for material adapted from *Visual Factfinder: Planet Earth* by Neil Curtis and Michael Allaby, copyright © Grisewood & Dempsey Ltd. 1993. Reprinted with permission of Larousse Kingfisher Chambers Inc., New York.

Luciano Picanco for line drawings.

Macmillan Education Australia for material from *The Geography Teacher's Guide to the Classroom* by John Fien, Rodney Gerber, and Peter Wilson. South Melbourne, Victoria, 1984.

McGraw-Hill for material from *Maps and Compasses: A User's Handbook* by Percy W. Blandford. © 1984 McGraw-Hill. Reproduced with permission of McGraw-Hill, Inc.

Prentice Hall for material from *World Geography* by H. H. Gross. Englewood Cliffs, New Jersey, 1980.

Reed Consumer Books Ltd. for material from *House of a Hundred Cats* by Irene Rawnsley.

Simon and Schuster Education Group for material from *Protecting Our Planet* by Ava Deutsch Drutman and Susan Klam Zuckerman. © 1991 by Good Apple, an imprint of Modern Curriculum, Simon & Schuster Elementary. Used by permission.

State News for material from Wednesday, January 11, 1995, Volume 90, No. 91.

Times Mirror Higher Education Group, Inc., for material from Arthur Getis, Judith Getis and Jerome Fellmann, *Introduction to Geography*, 3d ed. Copyright ©1991 Times Mirror Higher Education Group Inc., Dubuque, Iowa. All Rights Reserved. Reprinted by permission.

United Feature Syndicate for "Peanuts" reprinted by permission of United Feature Syndicate, Inc.

World Book, Inc., for material from *The Planet Earth,* Volume 4 of *The World Book Encyclopedia of Science.* © 1989 Verlagsgruppe Bertelsmann International. By permission of World Book, Inc.

To the Student

Welcome to *Earthbound!* There are several goals that this book sets forth for you.

It will help you improve your English skills and at the same time will introduce some basic concepts in geography. By the end of this course you will have information about the earth and other planets in the solar system. You will also study different aspects of human, technical, environmental, and, most importantly, physical geography. For example, you will learn about mountains, volcanoes, earthquakes, rivers, and the climate on Earth.

You will also learn much about the English language itself, since there is a focus in this book on improving your listening and reading comprehension as well as your ability to speak and write. By studying English while studying about the earth and the other planets in the solar system, you will have greater opportunities for learning.

Contents

Chapter 1. Defining Geography   1
- I.   What Is Geography?   4
- II.   The Four Fields of Geography   8

Chapter 2. Geographer's Tools: Maps and Globes   18
- I.   Interpreting Globes   21
- II.   Characteristics of Maps   28
- III.   Using Maps   35

Chapter 3. The Earth and Its Neighbors   43
- I.   The Sun's Family   46
- II.   Discovering Planet Earth   55

Chapter 4. The Earth in Stories   61
- I.   The Earth on Turtle's Back   63
- II.   Different Ideas about the Earth   73

Chapter 5. The Earth in Motion   83
- I.   Drifting Continental Plates   85
- II.   Earthquakes   93
- III.   When an Earthquake Hits!   101

Chapter 6. The Land   108
- I.   Mountains   112
- II.   Volcanoes   121
- III.   Living with Mountains and Volcanoes   128

Chapter 7. The Water   131
    I.   Oceans, Rivers, and Lakes of the World   135
    II.   The Different Faces of Water   137
    III.   Living with Water   142
    IV.   Water and Humans   147

Chapter 8. Weather and Climate   159
    I.   Weather Reports   161
    II.   Seasons and Climate   166
    III.   Living with the Climate   176

Appendixes   179
    A.   Pronunciation Chart   181
    B.   Units and Conversions   183
    C.   Directory of Environmental Organizations   185
    D.   Glossary   187

Chapter 1

Defining Geography

Geographers study the earth.

Do geographers only study the earth?

No! They also study how people live and work on the earth.

So geographers study the earth and geographers study the people on the earth?

Yes!

A Look Ahead

The title of this book is *Earthbound.* This word can have two meanings.

a. "not able to leave the earth" (human beings can only live on the earth)
b. "travel to the earth" (to visit the earth)

1

2 · Earthbound

The earth is the only place where human beings can live. Therefore, many people like to learn more about this planet, or to study it. This book lets the reader "visit the earth" and learn interesting things about this planet.

The study of the earth is called *geography*. You will learn what *geographers*, the people studying the earth, know about the earth and how to give this information in English. The first two chapters in the book prepare for the "visit" to this planet. Chapter 1 is about the word *geography*. This chapter explains what the word means and describes the different things that geographers study.

To the Student

At the end of this chapter, you will be able to

1. explain what geographers study;
2. distinguish between the four fields of geography; and
3. describe your country with geographical terms.

Vocabulary Development

In this section of each chapter you will check your vocabulary knowledge and practice the pronunciation of words. Read the following list of important words from chapter 1. If you already know the word, put a check mark (✓) in the space in front of the word. When you finish the chapter, return to this list. Mark all the new words you learned. Write down additional words that you learned. (The words that are italicized will be used in a pronunciation exercise that appears later in this chapter.)

__ geography	__ geographer	__ subject	__ topic
__ *country*	__ land	__ development	__ pollution
__ interview	__ teacher	__ student	__ *classroom*
__ *weather*	__ *water*	__ lake	__ river
__ people	__ place	__ city	__ village
__ question	__ *map*	__ industry	__ agriculture
__ cartography	__ draw	__ explain	__ describe
__ *study*	__ ask	__ *answer*	__ hear
__ use	__ repeat	__ read	__ work
__ *technical*	__ physical	__ small	__ big

Defining Geography · 3

_____	_____	_____	_____
_____	_____	_____	_____
_____	_____	_____	_____
_____	_____	_____	_____
_____	_____	_____	_____
_____	_____	_____	_____

The English language has many different sounds. There is a list with all the sounds in the English language in appendix A. When you look at that list, you will see that in English one letter can have different sounds. To help you learn the English sounds and other features of pronunciation, some chapters in this book will have a pronunciation practice at the beginning. Throughout your work on each chapter, keep the pronunciation focus for the chapter in mind.

The selected sounds for chapter 1 are

[æ] as in m*a*n or *a*sk   [ɑ] as in w*a*nt or f*a*rm
[e] as in b*e*d or g*e*t   [ʌ] as in wh*a*t or b*u*t

Listen especially for these sounds when you practice new words with your classmates and teacher. Look at the vocabulary list and find the italicized words that have one of the four sounds. Then write these words in the correct position in the chart that follows. When you are done with the chapter, try to add more words to this list.

[æ]	[e]	[ɑ]	[ʌ]
land			

4 · Earthbound

I. What Is Geography?

A. Complete the sentences about the picture. Use each of the words once.

classroom   subject   teacher   ask   geography   study

1. Diane is a _____.
2. She teaches _____.
3. She explains the _____ to the students.
4. The students _____ geography.
5. They are in the _____.
6. They _____ many questions.

B. In Activity A you used two kinds of words: *nouns* and *verbs*. What is the difference between a noun and a verb?

Nouns and Verbs

A *verb* tells what someone does or experiences.

    Verbs: teach   study   cry   fall

A *noun* is the name of a person, place, thing, or quality.

    Nouns: student   teacher   city   house
    Note: *Nouns* can be the subject or the object of a sentence.
        <u>The students</u> <u>study</u> <u>geography</u>.
          subject   + verb + object

Label each of the following words as either a noun or a verb, using the answer blanks that appear to the right of the words. (Some words could be both nouns and verbs.) Then give more examples of nouns and verbs. Two examples have been done for you.

teach	=	_verb_		teacher	=	_noun_
study	=	_____		geography	=	_____
classroom	=	_____		explain	=	_____
ask	=	_____		answer	=	_____
book	=	_____		subject	=	_____
_____	=	_____		_____	=	_____
_____	=	_____		_____	=	_____
_____	=	_____		_____	=	_____

C. Read the information in the accompanying language box and identify the *subject* (S), *verb* (V), and *object* (O) in the sentences following the language box. Write S, V, O in the correct position underneath each sentence. Some sentences may have more than one object.

Example:

Geographers study the earth.
     S   V   O

The Parts of the Simple Sentence

Subject (who or what the sentence is talking about)

    Geographers study the earth.
         S

Note: The subject of a sentence can be a *noun* or a *personal pronoun* (I, you, he, she, it, we, they).

    They study the earth.
     S

Verb (the action or experience described in the sentence)

    Geographers study the earth.
            V

> *The Parts of the Simple Sentence (continued)*
>
> *Object* (the person or thing that receives the action of the verb)
>
> >   Geographers study the earth.
> >   O
>
> *Note:* Not all sentences have an object.
>
> The English sentence also has a certain *format*. It should always include
>
> > a *capital letter* (A, B, C, . . .) at the beginning
> >   Geographers study the earth.
> >   Do geographers study the earth only?
>
> > a *punctuation mark* (. ? !) at the end
> >   Geographers study the earth.
> >   Do geographers study the earth only?

1. Geographers study different topics.

2. Geographers study the people.

3. Geographers describe people and places.

4. Some geographers draw maps.

5. Geographers use many different tools.

Defining Geography · 7

D. You will listen to an interview. The interviewer talks to a geography teacher. Her name is Diane Wayland. She teaches the subject "geography" at Roselake College in Michigan.

1. Close your books and listen to the interview. What is the interview about?

2. Listen to the interview again and fill in the blanks with the words you hear.

Interviewer: ___*Are*___ you a teacher at Roselake College?

Diane: Yes, I ___*am*___ a geography teacher.

Interviewer: Geography? Mmh, ___*Do*___ your students like this subject?

Diane: Yes, very much. Many students take geography classes.

Interviewer: Why ___*is*___ geography so interesting for the students?

Diane: Geography ___*is*___ a very useful subject in school. Students can learn many things about the whole world. They can also use geography in their daily life.

Interviewer: Mmh, I guess I ___*don't*___ really understand. What ___*does*___ the word *geography* actually mean?

Diane: The word *geography* ___*is*___ of Greek origin. It means "the study of the earth." Geographers study the earth and the people on the earth. This means that geographers study many different topics.

8 · **Earthbound**

    E. Are the following statements about the interview true or false? For each statement write true (T) or false (F) in the answer blank.

1. Diane is a geography teacher. <u>T</u>
2. The interviewer knows what the word *geography* means. ___
3. When you study geography, you study the earth and the people. ___
4. The students like the subject "geography." ___
5. *Geography* is a Spanish word. ___
6. All geographers study the same thing. ___

    F. Answer the three questions about geography. Tell a partner about your answers.

1. Do you remember your geography classes in school? What did you study in these classes?

2. Is it difficult to study geography? What do you like/not like about geography classes?

3. Is geography an important subject in school? Why is it/is it not important? When do you need geography?

II. The Four Fields of Geography

    A. In section I you listened to the beginning of the interview with Diane Wayland. Now listen to the rest of the interview.

1. First, listen to the interview and decide what it is about. Circle *a*, *b*, or *c*.

    a. The interview is about geography teachers at Roselake College.

Defining Geography · 9

    ✓ b. The interview is about the four fields of geography.
       c. The interview is about the problems in geography.

2. Now listen to the interview again and fill in the information in the chart that follows.

*[Margin notes: 2nd listening - write answers; 3rd listening - groups, overheads to each group, *more listenings as needed]*

Name of the Field	Topics
1. physical geo.	land, water, climate, mountains, volcanoes
2. environmental	dirty (polluted) air, water + land
3. human geo.	how people live + work
4. technical geo	developing maps, taking pictures

[Margin notes: groups — Viviane, Nana, Aumen (red); HoJin, SooJin, Hiro (green); Naoko, Abelardo, Sayaka (black); Masa, Yukio, HoSin (red); JinYoung, Abdalaziz, Atsu (blue)]

3. Listen to the interview again and fill in the words that you hear.

[Margin note: Final listening - pairs, √ answers, practice the interview]

Interviewer: You said that geographers study very different things, or topics. I heard that there ___are___ four big areas, or fields, in geography. Could you explain what the ___four___ fields in geography are?

Diane: Well, the ___study___ of geography is sometimes divided into four fields, that's correct. Let me give you the names of all fields. I will also ___explain___ what the people in these areas study, or what the different topics in each field are.

Interviewer: ___Is___ one of the fields physical geography?

Diane: Yes. The oldest field is physical geography. In physical geography you study the ___water___, the ___land___, and the climate. You study mountains, volcanoes, and earthquakes but also rivers, lakes, and oceans, and you learn how they affect the __weather__.

Interviewer: But today we __have__ problems with the land, the water, and the air. All these things __are__ dirty. Our environment is polluted. Who studies environmental problems?

Diane: There is a new field for the study of the environment. It is called environmental geography. People in this area study things like air pollution or water __pollution__.

Interviewer: Okay.

Diane: The __3rd__ field of geography is related to environmental geography. It is called __human__ geography. Do you __have__ any idea what these geographers study?

Interviewer: Well, I guess they study human beings.

Diane: Yup, that's a good start. They study how people __live__ together, what languages they speak, and where they live.

Interviewer: Oh, okay. What about the fourth field?

Diane: The fourth field is called technical geography. Geographers in this field must work on the development of all kinds of __maps__.

Interviewer: Oh, cartography?

Diane: Yes, exactly. Cartography __is__ the study of maps. But it is only one part of technical geography. Technical geography also includes things like satellite pictures of the earth.

B. Diane says in the interview that geography includes four different fields. Following are a blank chart and a list of things that geographers study. Try to put these topics into one of the four fields listed in the chart (sometimes a topic may fit into more than one field). Two examples have been done for you. Why do you think a particular topic should belong in one field and not in another field?

pairs

weather	mountain	cartography
volcano	ocean	houses
city	water pollution	cultural differences
agriculture	globes	industry
climate	population growth	unemployment
map	weather forecast	satellite pictures of the earth

Physical Geography	Environmental Geography	Human Geography	Technical Geography
			satellite pictures of the earth
volcano			

C. Write five sentences about your country. In each sentence use at least one of the words given in the following list. Then write down the field of geography for the sentence. An example has been done for you.

individuals

big	small	cold	warm	language	people
country	village	city	rain	weather	pollution
lake	ocean	river	volcano	mountain	

Example:

China is a very big country.
physical geography

1. _____
   _____
   _____

2. _____
   _____
   _____

3. _____
   _____
   _____

4. _____
   _____
   _____

5. _____
   _____
   _____

D. An important part of an interview is how you ask for information. Look at two questions (1 and 2) from the interview with Diane Wayland. Go back to the interview on page 7, find the answers Diane gave, and write them on the blank lines. In what ways are the two questions different? (*Hint:* What kinds of words are used? How do you answer the questions?)

Defining Geography · 13

Question 1.
Do your students like this subject?

Answer: _____

Question 2.
What does the word *geography* actually mean?

Answer: _____

Yes/No Questions

This type of question is called a *yes/no question* because you only have to answer *yes* or *no*.

Yes/no questions are formed with *do* or *does* + main verb.

    Do your students *like* geography?   Yes, they do./No, they don't.
    Does the teacher *like* geography?   Yes, she does./No, he doesn't.

If the verb of the sentence is a form of *to be*, do not add the auxiliary *to do*.

    Are you a teacher at Roselake College?   Yes, I am./No, I'm not.
    Is one of the fields physical geography?   Yes, it is./No, it isn't.

Wh Questions

This type of question is called a *wh question* because almost all of the words at the beginnings of these questions start with *wh*. You use these questions when you ask for more information and you want a longer answer. Therefore, some people also call this type of question an *information question*.

Wh questions are formed with a *question word* + *do* + subject (S) + *main verb* (V).

    What do the students *like* about geography?
                S + V

    Why do the students *study* geography?
                S + V

Wh Questions (continued)

When the verb of the sentence is a form of *to be*, do not add the auxiliary *to do*.

Why is geography so interesting?   *What are* the four fields of geography?

When the question word is the *subject* of the sentence, do not use a form of *to do*.

Who studies environmental problems?
  S   V

She studies environmental problems.
  S   V

How do you ask for information?

Use *why* to ask about a reason.   Use *who* to ask about a person.
Use *what* to ask about a thing.   Use *where* to ask about a place.

E. Write down five questions that you would like to ask your classmates about their home countries/hometowns. Walk around the classroom and find the answers to your questions. Try to ask as many people as you can. Write the answers next to your questions and note the name of the person you asked.

Example:

Wh Questions

Question 1. Where do you come from?

Answer: Taiwan (Chia Fen)
          South Korea (Jennifer)

Question 2. What is the name of the capital city?

Answer: Taipei (Chia Fen)
          Seoul (Jennifer)

Yes/No Questions

Question 3. Are the rivers in your country dirty?

Answer: Yes (Jordi)
          Yes (Heidi)

Question 4. Do you live in a big city?

Answer: No (Lisa)
          No (Han)

Question 1. _____

      Answer (name): _____

      _____

      _____

Question 2. _____

      Answer (name): _____

      _____

      _____

16 · Earthbound

Question 3. _____

      Answer (name): _____

                              _____

                              _____

Question 4. _____

      Answer (name): _____

                              _____

                              _____

Question 5. _____

      Answer (name): _____

                              _____

                              _____

F. Now write one sentence (or more if you have more information) about each person in your class.

Examples:

      Chia Fen is from Taiwan.
      Han does not live in a big city. He lives in a small village.

Defining Geography · 17

G. This activity helps you review the vocabulary you learned in this chapter. Twenty words from the chapter are hidden in the box. Look from left to right and top to bottom. When you find a word, draw a circle around it. The first word has been done for you.

```
E D F G E X P L A I N I L U K S C O U N T R Y D
N D R L I V E R U H P O L L U T I O N I T R Q E
V D I F F E R E N T H T M D T U E R J N X W L V
I H G E O G R A P H Y A L S E D B U L T S E I E
R U S W D D I R T Y S D F V L Y D E R E L A P L
O M W P G I A T E V I L L A G E P A B R B T E O
N A A E H Y R H S P C T O O U T T E I V K H V P
M N T O P I C I R L A T Y K V B I I E I E E V M
E P N P E N T P I U L G U A I P B I M E W R S E
N P S L H U M F C A R T O G R A P H Y W O G E N
T G V E U N E M P L O Y M E N T L D E N E P L T
```

Chapter 2

Geographer's Tools: Maps and Globes

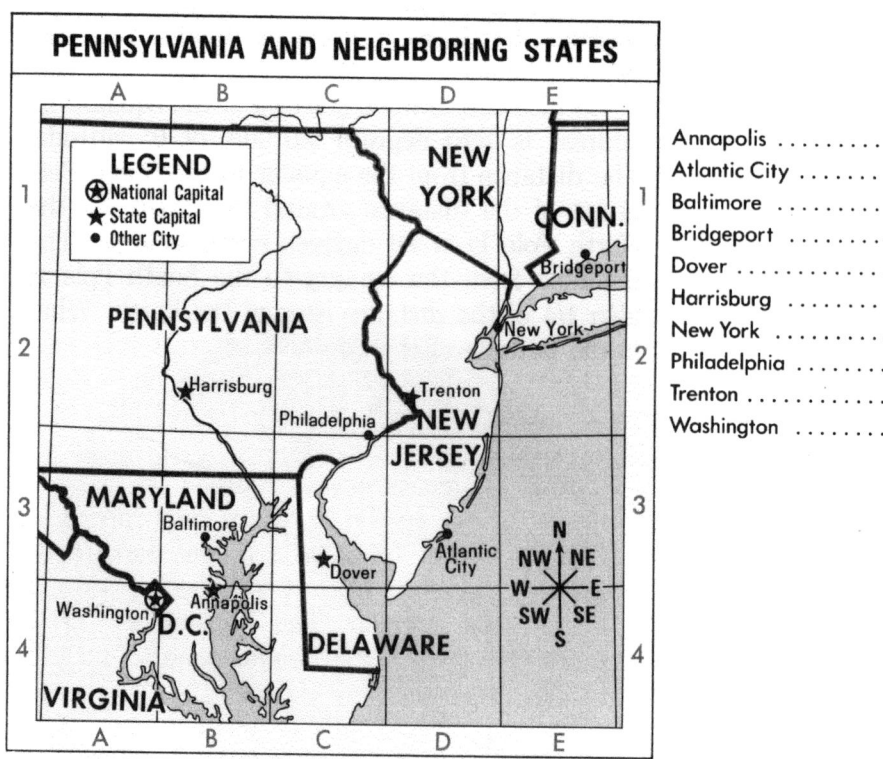

From A. Graham and R. Thomas, *Discovering Maps: A Young Person's World Atlas* (Maplewood, NJ: Hammond, Inc. 1991). © Hammond Incorporated, Maplewood, New Jersey, license #12,275.

Geographer's Tools · 19

A Look Behind/A Look Ahead

Chapter 1 showed the different fields of geography. If you want to understand the work in these different fields, it is often necessary to work with the tools that geographers use. Therefore, this chapter will focus on two very important tools in the study of the earth—maps and globes. Geographers use maps and globes for many different reasons and in many different ways. In this chapter we will focus only on physical maps and will see how geographers use them to show the locations of countries, oceans, rivers, mountains, cities, or buildings. Another important goal of this chapter is to practice making maps and to learn how to read maps that other people have made.

To the Student

At the end of this chapter, you will be able to

1. describe what you can see on a globe;
2. read maps by understanding the information presented in maps;
3. use latitude and longitude to find a location on a map;
4. understand time zones; and
5. draw your own maps.

Vocabulary Development

Read the following list of important words from chapter 2 (you may have seen some of them in chapter 1). If you already know the word, put a check mark (✓) in the space in front of the word. When you finish the chapter, return to this list. Mark all the new words you learned. Write down additional words that you learned. (The words that are italicized here will be used in an exercise that appears later in the chapter.)

___ *school*	___ map key	___ *floor* plan	___ distance
___ grid	___ *cross*	___ center	___ equator
___ *globe*	___ top	___ symbol	___ information
___ railroad	___ meridian	___ scale	___ area *code*
___ building	___ direction	___ address	___ shopping center
___ *road*	___ street	___ time *zone*	___ capital
___ explain	___ look	___ *draw*	___ read

20 · Earthbound

__ *for*   __ bottom   __ *longitude*   __ *latitude*
__ *lose*   __ measure   __ be *close* to   __ be far from

_____   _____   _____   _____

_____   _____   _____   _____

_____   _____   _____   _____

_____   _____   _____   _____

_____   _____   _____   _____

_____   _____   _____   _____

In this chapter, focus on the following sounds.

[ɔː] as in l*o*ng or b*a*ll   [əʊ] as in b*oa*t or n*o*

[uː] as in t*wo* or f*oo*d   [ʊ] as in g*oo*d or b*oo*k

Listen especially for these sounds when you practice new words with your classmates and teacher. Look at the vocabulary list and find the italicized words that have one of the four sounds. Then write these words in the correct position in the chart that follows. When you are done with the chapter, try to add more words to this list.

[ɔː]	[uː]	[əʊ]	[ʊ]

I. Interpreting Globes

A. Fill in the blanks in the following sentences. Use each word only once.

size   shape   divides   consists of
center   bottom   measure   globe

1. A _globe_ is a model of the earth.

2. The earth _consists of_ land and water.

3. Some fish swim very deep. These fish often live at the _bottom_ of the sea.

4. The _center_ of the earth is very hot.

5. To find the _size_ of a country you must _measure_ it.

6. The equator _divides_ the globe into a southern and a northern part.

7. A globe is usually round. In other words, it has a round _shape_.

B. Imagine that you are at the Museum of Geography. A speaker will give you a guided tour. Your tour group just entered the exhibition on modern globes. The tour guide will explain what you can see on a globe. While you are listening to the tour guide, look at the picture of the globe and use the following words to name the parts of the globe. (Write the words next to the globe.)

North Pole   South Pole   Northern Hemisphere
Southern Hemisphere   equator   parallel
meridian   prime meridian

① listen while I demonstrate
② listen in pairs & answer

22 · Earthbound

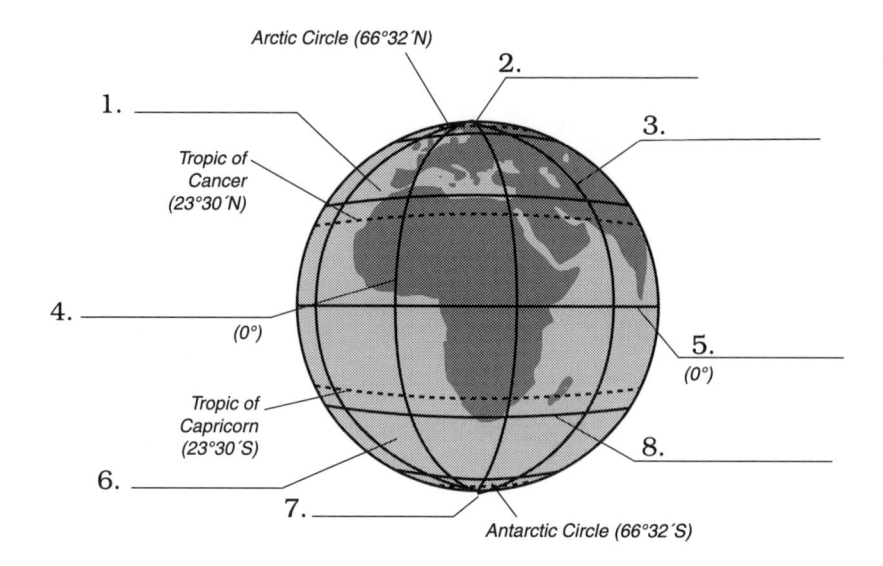

Diagram labels:
- 1. _____
- 2. _____ (Arctic Circle (66°32′N))
- 3. _____
- Tropic of Cancer (23°30′N)
- 4. _____ (0°)
- 5. _____ (0°)
- Tropic of Capricorn (23°30′S)
- 6. _____
- 7. _____ (Antarctic Circle (66°32′S))
- 8. _____

C. Try to answer the following questions with a partner. Then compare your results with those of your classmates.

1. What does the earth's surface consist of?
   land + water

2. What do you call the places at the top and the bottom of the globe?
   poles

3. Do you live in the Northern or the Southern Hemisphere?

4. Is Asia located in the Eastern or the Western Hemisphere?
   Eastern

5. What do you call the black lines on a globe?
   meridians + parallels

6. Look at a globe or a map and find the following cities. (*Note:* Latitude and longitude of these cities are not exact.)

   a. 51°N, 0° *London*

b. 36°N, 140°E _Tokyo_

c. 0°, 78°W _Quito_

d. 40°N, 105°W _Denver_

D. Listen to the presentation about globes again and take notes next to the globe on p. 22.

E. Read each of the following sentences and try to find the answers in your notes from Activity D. Circle the letter of the correct answer.

1. You can see the ____c____ of a body of water on the globe.

    a. size
    b. shape
    c. size and shape

2. The ____a____ is the line that goes through Greenwich, England.

    a. prime meridian
    b. equator
    c. hemisphere

3. When we measure the distance north or south of the equator, we talk about ____c____.

    a. longitude
    b. meridian
    c. latitude

4. Distances between meridians of longitude and parallels of latitude are measured in ____b____.

    a. meters
    b. degrees
    c. feet

24 · **Earthbound**

5. The prime meridian ____a____.

   a. was chosen by people during a conference in 1884
   b. is a natural line you can see on the ground
   c. is a black line you can see when you go to England

6. The lines north and south of the equator are called parallels because ____a____.

   a. they never cross
   b. they are imaginary
   c. they divide the earth

7. The equator is an ____b____ line around the middle of the earth.

   a. imagine
   b. imaginary
   c. image

8. You need longitude and latitude to find the ____c____ of a place.

   a. lines
   b. locate
   c. location

F. When you look at a globe, you can easily see the shapes of those countries that have water around them. With a partner try to name all the countries in the pictures. Write their names in the first column of the chart on page 26. Then fill in the rest of the chart with the other information. (*Hint:* All of the countries are bordered by water on some of their boundaries.)

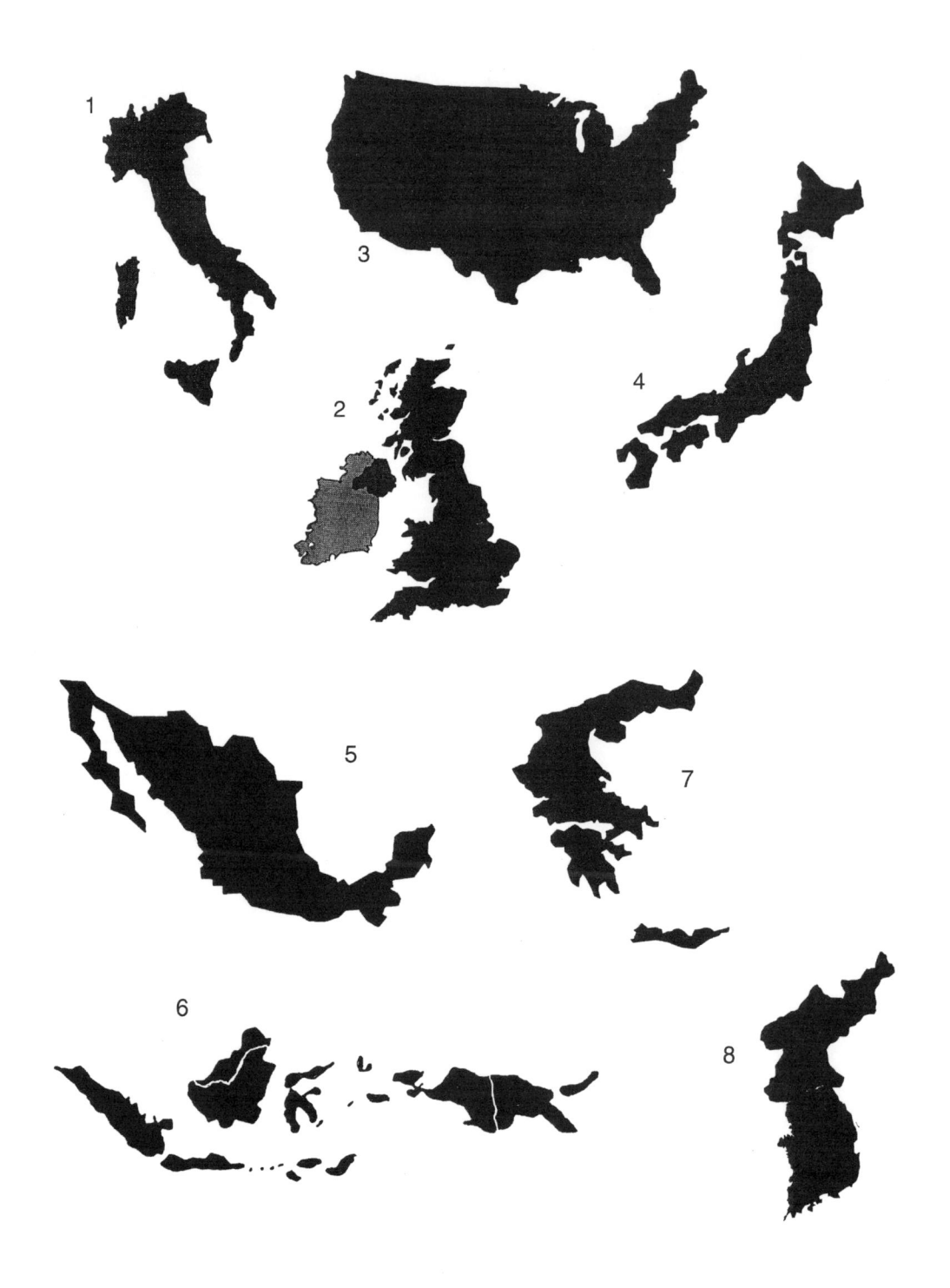
1
3
4
2
5
7
6
8

Earthbound

	Country	Nationality	Language
1.			
2.			
3.			
4.			
5.			
6.			
7.			
8.			

G. Latitude and longitude are necessary to find the location of a place on globes or maps. But this is not the only reason why we need the grid system. Latitude can tell us something about the weather in a country (see chap. 8), and longitude can tell us something about the local time in a country. The map "The Time around the World" on p. 27 shows the meridians of longitude. They are the basis for the world time zones. Look at the map and answer the following questions about the time zones.

1. Find the prime meridian in the picture. At how many degrees longitude do you find this line on a map? 0°

2. Find the international date line. 180° longitude

3. What do you think *international date line* means? imaginary line thru Pacific Ocean — east of the line is one day earlier

4. Each time zone is about 15° wide. What meridian does the international date line follow? 180° long.

5. What is the time difference between India and the West Coast of the United States? 13 hours

Geographer's Tools · 27

6. It is noon in New York City (Sunday, December 31st). What day of the week is it in Australia?   *Monday Jan. 1*

The Time around the World

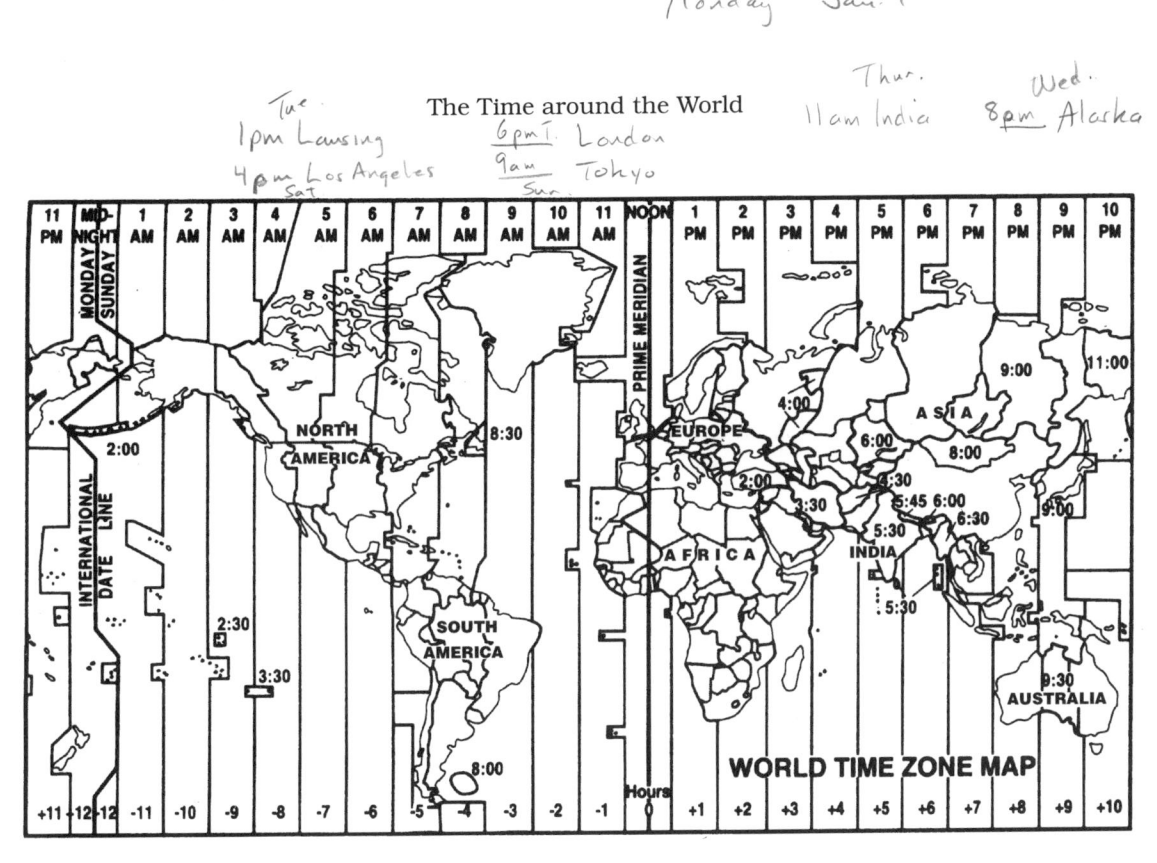

Tue.
1pm Lansing
4pm Los Angeles
Sat

6pm London
9am Tokyo
Sun

Thur.
11am India

Wed.
8pm Alaska

© R. R. Donnelley & Sons Co. 1993

H. Read the clues and fill in the words in the crossword puzzle on p. 28.

Across
1. Manhattan, Singapore, Lagos (the capital of Nigeria), and Montreal all have one thing in common. Each is located on an _____.
2. The _____ is a model of the earth.
3. the line that divides the earth into a Northern and a Southern Hemisphere
4. When it is summer in the Southern Hemisphere, it is _____ in the Northern Hemisphere.
5. A road with houses or other buildings on both sides is called a _____.

28 · **Earthbound**

Down
6. The largest continent in the world is _____.
7. A _____ is usually between towns. It is an open way for vehicles to travel on.
8. From this big city in the United States (located in the Midwest) you can drive south to enter Canada.
9. A different word for *number* is _____.
10. the name of a country that is located on two continents
11. Geographers study the _____.

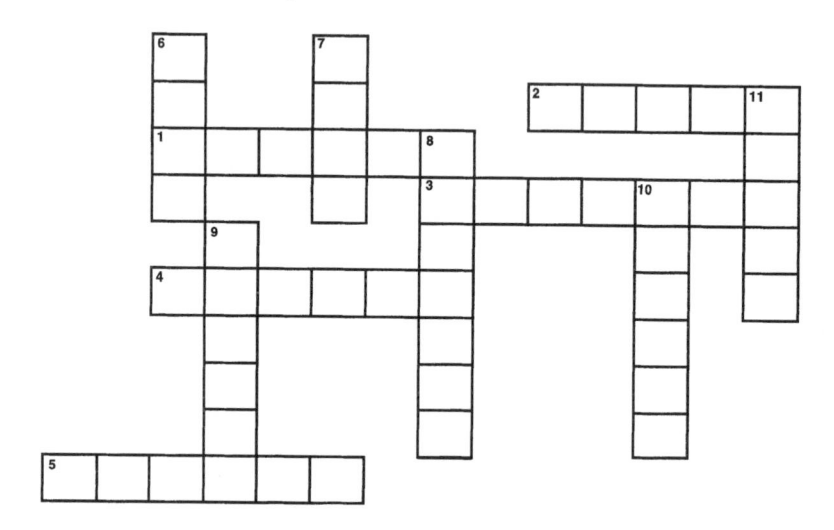

II. Characteristics of Maps

A. Look at the cartoon. What is it about? Why doesn't Snoopy (the dog) like the map?

PEANUTS® by Charles M. Schulz

"Peanuts" reprinted by permission of United Feature Syndicate, Inc.

Geographer's Tools · 29

B. There are many different types of maps. Sometimes they have different names. With a partner, answer the following questions about maps. When you are done, compare your answers with those of your classmates.

1. What kinds of maps can you think of?

2. When and where do you use them?

3. How do you know what a map is about? Where can you find this information on the map?

C. Read the paragraph "Names for Maps." Then find the italicized words in the text and match each with the correct picture.

NAMES FOR MAPS

There are many different types of maps. The type of map that a cartographer draws depends on what he or she wants to show. For example, a *political map* shows the locations of boundaries and the locations of cities. A physical map shows the elevation of land, the courses of rivers or streams, and other details of the land. Elevations, or mountain areas, can be shown in different ways. Many maps use different colors to identify the height of an area. Other ways of showing elevations are *cross-sections* and *contour maps*. If a map shows a fairly small area and gives a fairly big representation of it, it is no longer called a map. Such drawings are called plans. So you will hear people talk about a city map or a road map, but when they are talking about the town center, they will use the word "plan." A drawing of the rooms in a building is also never called a floor map. It is called a *floor plan*.

30 · Earthbound

a. _____

b. _____

c. _____

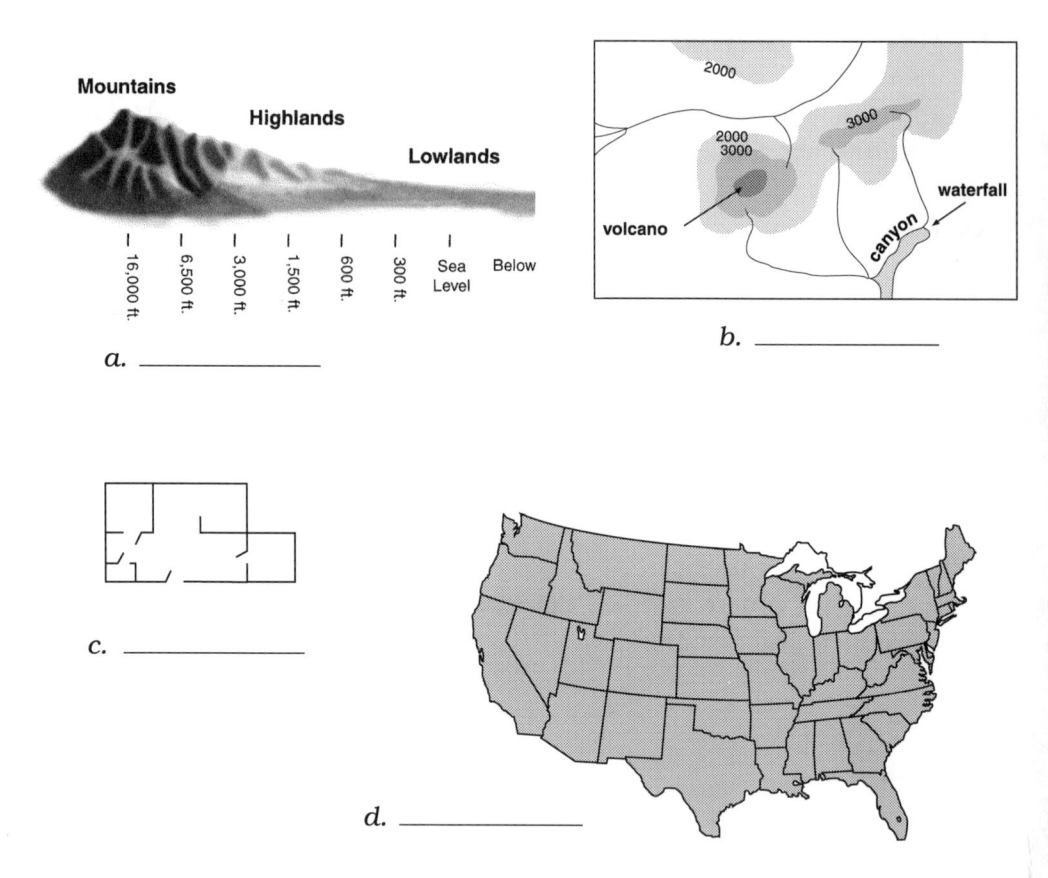

d. _____

D. It is impossible to draw a picture of the real world. Therefore, a map uses *symbols* to represent real world objects. Read the passage about a special symbol on political maps. Unfortunately, the writer made mistakes in capitalization (10 mistakes) and punctuation (4 mistakes). Try to find the mistakes and correct them.

Cartographers present information with the help of globes and maps. they use different symbols for different types of information The symbols are often explained in the map key. check the keys to the maps you use for this chapter. You will probably find a special symbol for Capital Cities like washington, DC, the capital of the United States, or Columbus, the capital of ohio The capital is the center of the government maps usually mark it with a special symbol. On your map cities like Paris, the capital of france, or Ottawa, the capital of canada, should all have symbols by their names. do you know the name of the highest capital city in the world.

Geographer's Tools · 31

STATE OF OHIO

FIVE CITIES OF NORTHEAST OHIO

From A. Graham and R. Thomas, *Discovering Maps: A Young Person's World Atlas* (Maplewood, NJ: Hammond, Inc. 1991). © Hammond Incorporated, Maplewood, New Jersey, license #12,275.

E. Here are some map keys with other symbols that are commonly used on road maps and city maps. Write the letter of the correct symbol in the answer blank next to its description.

Descriptions:
railroad _o_   school _h_   rapids _d_   windmill _i_   picnic area _p_
campground _k_   swamp _c_   food _l_   lake _b_   visitor center _m_
dam with road _e_   river or stream _a_   parking _j_   mine _f_
church _g_   boat ramp _q_   medical service _n_

Symbols Representing Water

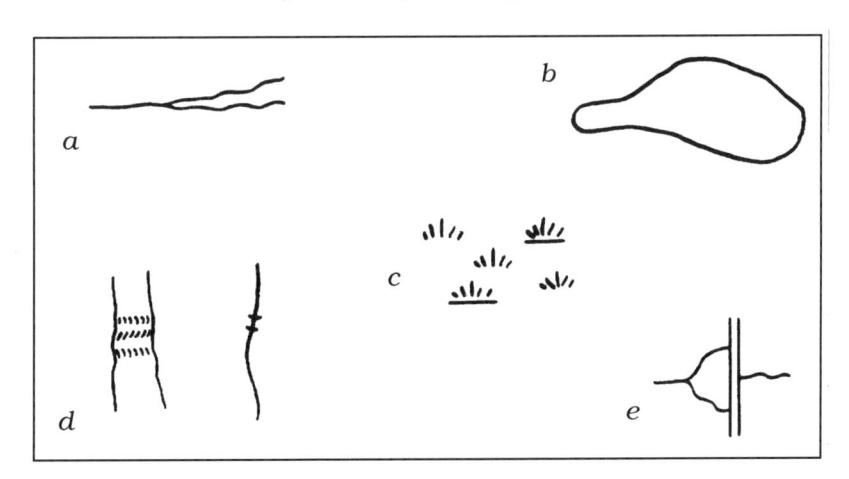

Symbols for Isolated Landmark Features

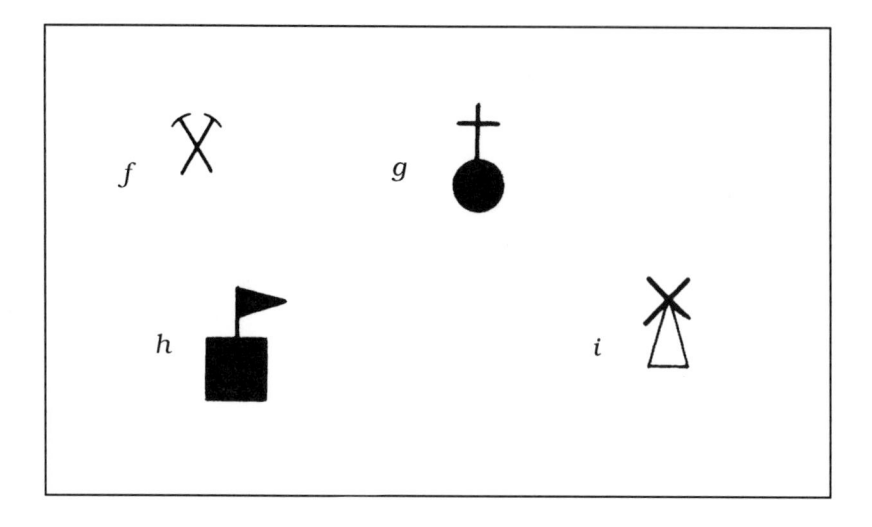

f ⛏ *g* � *h* 🚩 *i* 🌬

Symbols Used for Maps of Recreational Areas

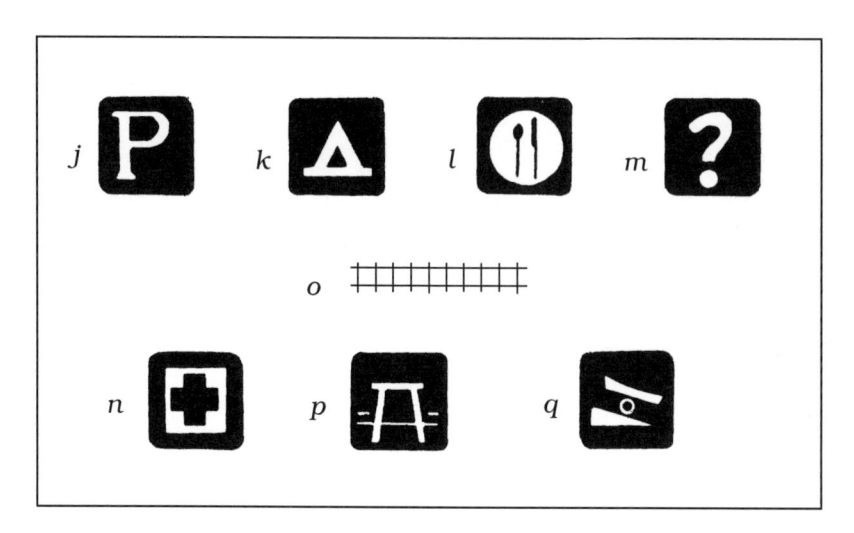

j P *k* ▲ *l* 🍴 *m* ?

o ╫╫╫╫╫

n ✚ *p* 🪑 *q* ⛵

Symbols from Percy W. Blandford, *Maps and Compasses: A User's Handbook* (Blue Ridge Summit, PA: McGraw-Hill, 1984).

F. Two important characteristics of maps are their purpose and the symbols that are used to show the information. There are, however, more parts of a map that one needs to know about to be able to interpret the map correctly. Answer the following questions about the map on p. 34.

Geographer's Tools · 33

1. What is the purpose of the map? What does it show?

2. How do you know where north and south are on the map?

3. Is Flint (G-4) located east or west of Grand Rapids (G-2)?

4. Is the city of Muskegon north or south of Holland? (*Hint:* Both towns are located on the eastern shore of Lake Michigan.)

5. How do you know how big the real area is?

6. How many miles/kilometers are shown by 1/2 inch on the map that shows the Upper Peninsula of Michigan?

7. How far is it from Grand Rapids (G-2) to Detroit (H-5)?

8. What is the name of the biggest city in Michigan? Where is it located?

9. What is the capital of the state of Michigan? How do you know?

10. Is there a highway that goes directly from Saginaw (G-4) to Detroit (H-5)?

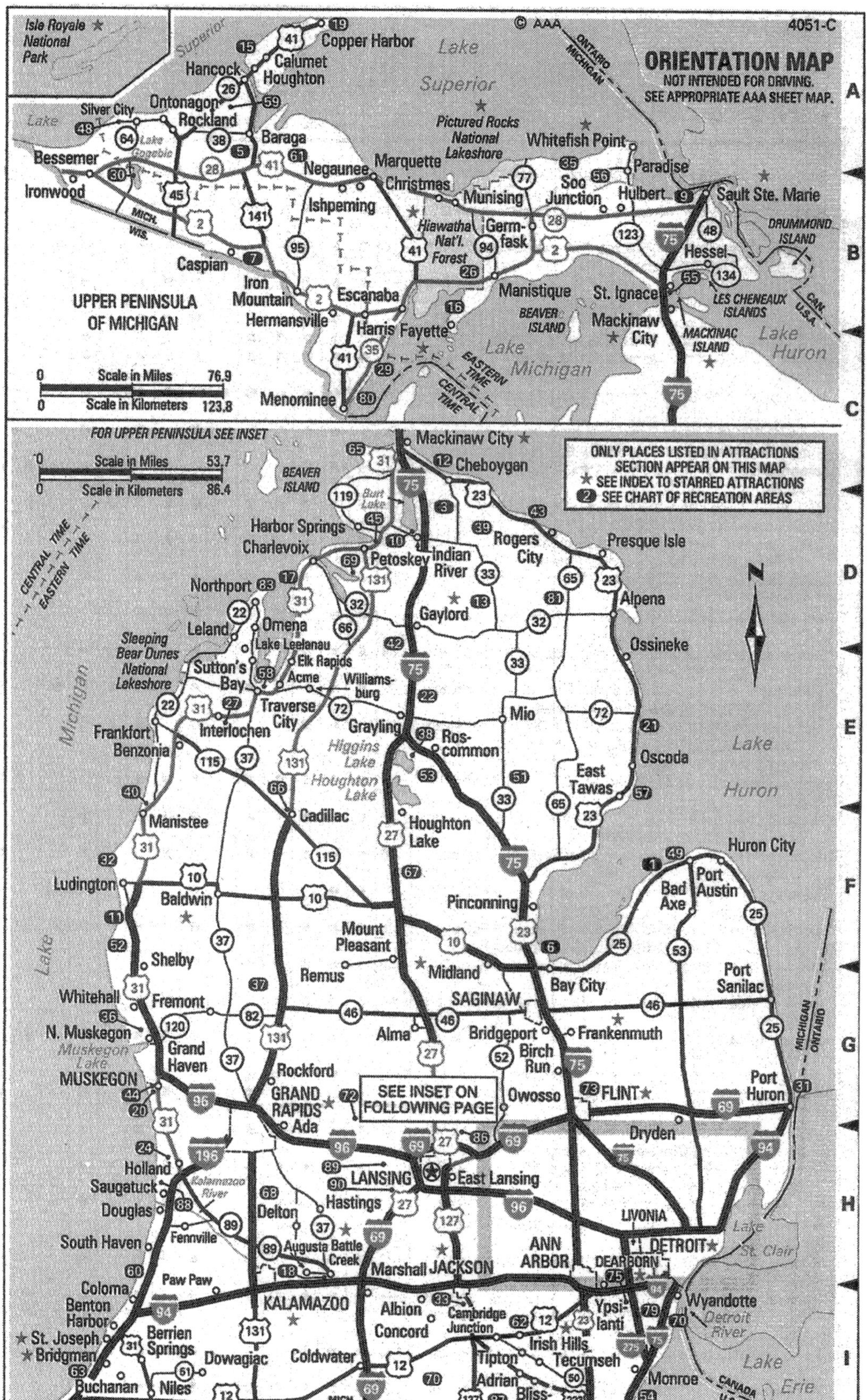
© AAA
4051-C
ORIENTATION MAP
NOT INTENDED FOR DRIVING.
SEE APPROPRIATE AAA SHEET MAP.
Isle Royale National Park
Lake Superior
Copper Harbor
Calumet
Hancock
Houghton
Ontonagon
Silver City
Rockland
Baraga
Lake Gogebic
Bessemer
Ironwood
Negaunee
Marquette
Christmas
Ishpeming
Pictured Rocks National Lakeshore
Whitefish Point
Paradise
Munising
Soo Junction
Hulbert
Sault Ste. Marie
Hiawatha Nat'l. Forest
Germfask
Hessel
DRUMMOND ISLAND
Caspian
Iron Mountain
Escanaba
Manistique
St. Ignace
LES CHENEAUX ISLANDS
UPPER PENINSULA OF MICHIGAN
Hermansville
Harris
Fayette
BEAVER ISLAND
Mackinaw City
MACKINAC ISLAND
Lake Huron
Lake Michigan
EASTERN TIME
CENTRAL TIME
ONTARIO
MICHIGAN
MICH.
WIS.
CAN.
U.S.A.
Menominee
Scale in Miles 0 76.9
Scale in Kilometers 0 123.8
FOR UPPER PENINSULA SEE INSET
Scale in Miles 0 53.7
Scale in Kilometers 0 86.4
ONLY PLACES LISTED IN ATTRACTIONS SECTION APPEAR ON THIS MAP
SEE INDEX TO STARRED ATTRACTIONS
SEE CHART OF RECREATION AREAS
Mackinaw City
Cheboygan
Burt Lake
Harbor Springs
Charlevoix
Petoskey
Indian River
Rogers City
Presque Isle
Northport
Alpena
Leland
Omena
Gaylord
Lake Leelanau
Elk Rapids
Ossineke
Sleeping Bear Dunes National Lakeshore
Sutton's Bay
Acme
Williamsburg
Traverse City
Mio
Frankfort
Benzonia
Interlochen
Grayling
Roscommon
Higgins Lake
Houghton Lake
Oscoda
East Tawas
Manistee
Cadillac
Houghton Lake
Huron City
Port Austin
Bad Axe
Ludington
Baldwin
Pinconning
Mount Pleasant
Shelby
Remus
Midland
Bay City
Port Sanilac
Whitehall
Fremont
SAGINAW
N. Muskegon
Muskegon Lake
Alma
Bridgeport
Frankenmuth
Grand Haven
Birch Run
MUSKEGON
Rockford
GRAND RAPIDS
SEE INSET ON FOLLOWING PAGE
Owosso
FLINT
Port Huron
Ada
Dryden
Holland
LANSING
East Lansing
Saugatuck
Kalamazoo River
Hastings
Douglas
Delton
LIVONIA
South Haven
Fennville
Augusta
Battle Creek
ANN ARBOR
DETROIT
DEARBORN
Lake St. Clair
Coloma
Paw Paw
Marshall
JACKSON
Benton Harbor
KALAMAZOO
Albion
Cambridge Junction
Ypsilanti
Wyandotte
Detroit River
St. Joseph
Bridgman
Berrien Springs
Concord
Irish Hills
Dowagiac
Coldwater
Tipton
Tecumseh
Adrian
Buchanan
Niles
Blissfield
Monroe
Lake Erie
CANADA
U.S.A.
MICH.
IND.
OHIO
MICHIGAN
ONTARIO
CENTRAL TIME
EASTERN TIME
Lake Michigan
A
B
C
D
E
F
G
H
I
1
2
3
4
5
6

[Handwritten notes at top:]
1. Listen - answer ?s
2. B. Listen
3. Listen - follow the directions

Geographer's Tools · 35

III. Using Maps

A. Two classmates meet on their first day of class. Look at the map and listen to the conversation between Rukiye and her classmate Mayu. What are Mayu and Rukiye talking about?

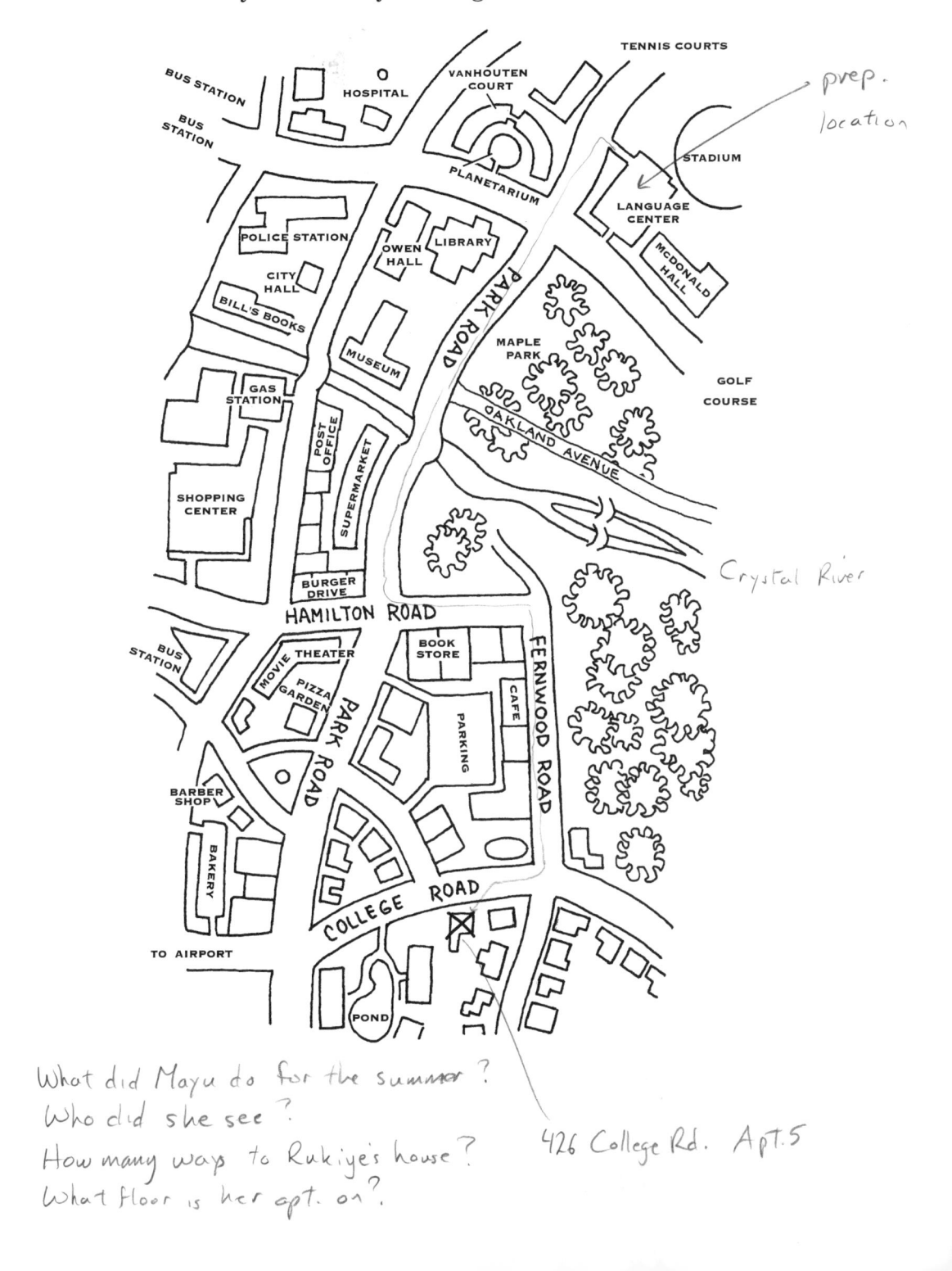

[Map of a town showing various locations including Bus Stations, Hospital, Vanhouten Court, Tennis Courts, Planetarium, Stadium, Language Center, Police Station, Owen Hall, Library, McDonald Hall, City Hall, Bill's Books, Museum, Maple Park, Golf Course, Gas Station, Post Office, Supermarket, Oakland Avenue, Shopping Center, Burger Drive, Hamilton Road, Movie Theater, Book Store, Pizza Garden, Park Road, Cafe, Parking, Fernwood Road, Barber Shop, Bakery, College Road, Pond, To Airport]

[Handwritten annotations on map:]
- prep. location (pointing to Language Center area)
- Crystal River (pointing to river)
- 426 College Rd. Apt. 5

[Handwritten questions at bottom:]
What did Mayu do for the summer?
Who did she see?
How many ways to Rukiye's house?
What floor is her apt. on?

B. When you explain a map to another person, you need special words to express *direction* or *distance*.

> How do I get *to* your house?

These words are called *prepositions*. They are short but very important words in the English language.

Prepositions

Use	Preposition	Example
direction	to	Go *to* the next traffic light.
distance	for	Continue *for* two blocks.
place	on/at	Turn right *on* Grand River Avenue.
		Turn right *at* the corner of Jolly and Saginaw.

1. Listen to Rukiye's explanation again and fill in the missing prepositions.

   Mayu: I'd love to see it! How do I get there?

   Rukiye: Oh, it's really easy. There are actually two ways to get (1) _To_ my house, but let me explain the nice walk along the park. Leave the Language Center through the Park Road entrance and turn left. Then go straight (2) _on_ Park Road. Cross Oakland Avenue and after about half a block cross Crystal River. Keep walking until you get (3) _to_ Hamilton Drive. Take a left (4) _at_ Hamilton and walk up (5) _To_ Fernwood. On Fernwood take a right and keep walking (6) _for_ about a quarter of a mile. Turn right (7) _at_ the corner of Fernwood and College Road. My house is the second (8) _on_ your left. The address is 426 College Road, Apt. 5. You have to walk all the way (9) _to_ the top floor of the building.

   Mayu: Thanks for the description. I'll see you tonight at around 7 then. Bye.

2. Look at Rukiye's explanation again. Do all the sentences have a subject?

Imperative

To give directions and instructions or to give a command or make a request, English speakers use the *imperative*. The *imperative* uses the base form of the verb. This is the form of the verb that you find in the dictionary; for example, *go, stop, turn*. In an imperative sentence we do not write or say the subject.

	Affirmative		*Negative*
~~You~~	*Go* to the next traffic light.	~~You~~	*Don't go* to the next traffic light.
	Continue for two blocks.		*Don't continue* for two blocks.
	Turn right on Grand River Avenue.		*Don't turn* right on Grand River Avenue.

C. Find a partner and go back to the map in Activity A. Ask your partner to choose a place on the map and to explain to you where it is. Tell your partner to start at that place and to follow your directions to a different location on the map. Don't tell your partner the name of the place he or she is going to. See if your partner can follow your directions.

D. Take out a piece of paper and draw a map that shows how to get from your school or workplace to your home. When you are done, give this map to a classmate. Explain to your classmate how to get to your house. Use important buildings or roads to help your classmate find your house.

38 · **Earthbound**

"Which way is up?"

E. After you have given your map to your classmate, think about the following questions. Based on your ideas and on your partner's suggestions, make the necessary corrections to your map.

1. How did you start drawing the map?

2. Where did you end?

3. Did you use any *symbols?*

4. Were all the buildings and streets the correct size or length in relation to each other?

F. When you open a U.S. phone book, you will find another very important map. This map shows the time zones in the United States. It also shows the area code you have to dial if you want to call a friend in a different state. You and your classmates will *scan* this map for information.

> *Scanning*
>
> In this chapter you practice how to quickly find information on a map. To do this successfully, you don't want to look at every single piece of information in the map. In the same way, when you open the phone book, you are only looking for one specific detail, a phone number, and you don't read the whole book. There are many other instances when you are just looking for one piece of information and you don't want to read the whole text. This form of reading is called *scanning*. Scanning is a very useful skill for reading. It means that you read very fast without reading every word.

Take three minutes to answer five questions about the area code map on page 40.

Questions

1. How many time zones are there in the United States?

2. Give the names of two time zones.

3. Do all people in Tennessee live in the same time zone?

4. Is the state of Oregon on the east coast or the west coast?

5. How many different area codes are there in Florida?

G. Look at the area code map and answer the following questions.

1. It is 3:00 P.M. in Chicago. What time is it in San Francisco?

    1 pm

2. It is 8:00 A.M. in Boston, Massachusetts. What time is it in Dallas, Texas?

    7 am

3. When you fly from the east to the west, do you lose time or do you gain time?

    gain

4. You take a plane from New York to Los Angeles. The flight time is six hours. You leave New York at 4:00 A.M. What is the time of your arrival in Los Angeles?

    7 am

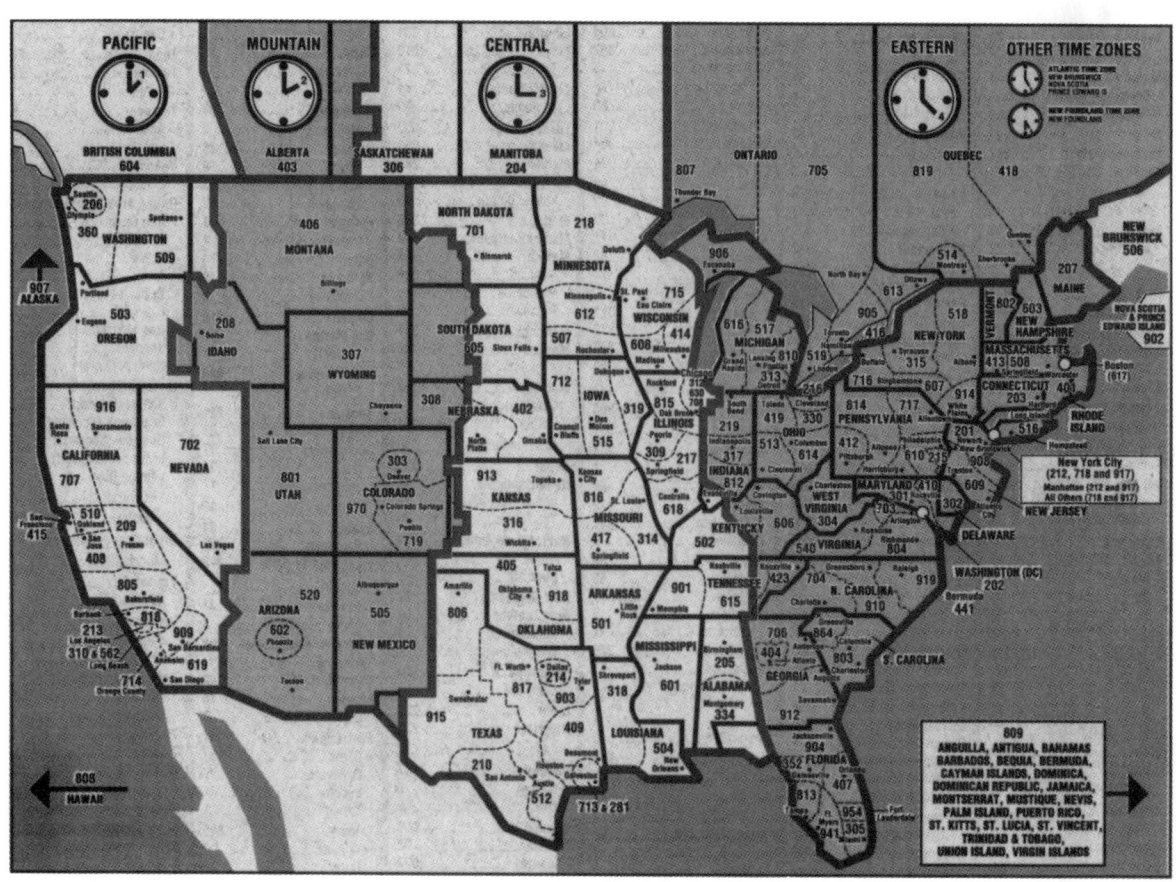

© Ameritech 1996.

5. What is the area code for Hawaii?   808

6. What is the area code for Omaha, Nebraska?   402

H. With a partner think about the following questions and report your results to the rest of the class.

1. People often say that maps are like pictures taken from high above or from outer space. Such pictures from high in the air are called aerial photographs. What kind of information can you find in maps that you cannot find in aerial photographs?

2. Cartographers often use colors to show important information. What colors would you use to present the following information on a map?

    a. tropical forests

    b. deserts

    c. mountains

    d. icebergs

3. You are planning a hiking trip to the Grand Canyon in Arizona. Give two reasons why you should take a physical map on your trip.

4. You expect a group of foreign teachers at your school. They are going to teach geography classes, but the problem is that they don't know the school building or the town very well. What kinds of maps do you need to get for them?

5. In the geography course these foreign teachers will talk about the mountains in the United States. They will discuss the Rocky Mountains in the western part of the United States and the Appalachian Mountains in the eastern part of the United States. What kinds of maps (they should show the mountain ranges and the flat area between them clearly) are you going to order for the class?

Chapter 3

The Earth and Its Neighbors

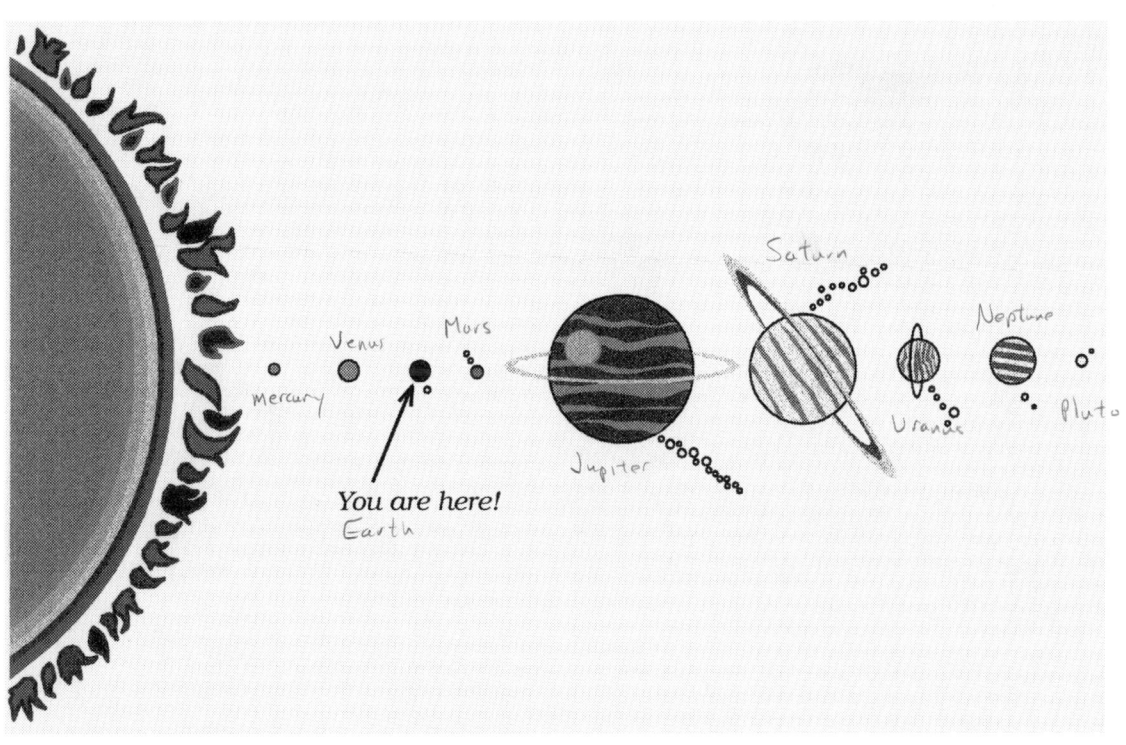

1. What can you see in this picture?
2. Do you know the names of any planets?

44 · Earthbound

A Look Behind/A Look Ahead

During the discussion of maps and globes in chapter 2, you learned that the earth is divided into bodies of water and bodies of land. This physical characteristic of the earth cannot be found on any of the other planets in the solar system. Do you think the earth is special in any other way?

The next three chapters of this book show how the earth is different from other planets, how people on earth started to observe and explain this planet, and what scientists today know about the physical characteristics of the earth. Chapter 3 begins with an introduction to our solar system and shows how the earth is different from other planets in this system. The last part of this chapter gives an example of one early geographer and shows how the first information about the earth was found.

To the Student

At the end of this chapter, you will be able to

1. identify the planets and talk about the solar system;
2. explain why the earth is different from other planets in the solar system; and
3. understand the beginnings of modern geography.

Vocabulary Development

Read the following list of important words from chapter 3 (you may have seen some of them in previous chapters). If you already know the word, put a check mark (✓) in the space in front of the word. When you finish the chapter, return to this list. Mark all the new words you learned. Write down additional words that you learned.

__ star	__ galaxy	__ planet	__ universe
__ soil	__ land	__ continent	__ distance
__ radius	__ average	__ diameter	__ compare
__ describe	__ consist of	__ freeze	__ grow
__ revolve	__ axis	__ rotate	__ turn
__ live	__ hot	__ far	__ close
__ cold	__ big	__ large	__ small

The Earth and Its Neighbors · 45

_____ _____ _____ _____

_____ _____ _____ _____

_____ _____ _____ _____

_____ _____ _____ _____

_____ _____ _____ _____

This chapter will not present sounds of the English language but will show a way to make it easier to pronounce new words. In English, all words have one or more *syllables*. A syllable is a word or a part of a word that has a *vowel* (*a, e, i, o, u*). When you learn a new word, it helps to pronounce one syllable at a time. If you are not sure how many syllables there are, check the dictionary. The dictionary usually marks syllables with a dot ( ) or a hyphen (-).

Example:

The word *Earth* has one syllable:	*Earth*	[ɜrθ]
The word *country* has two syllables:	*coun | try*	[kʌn|tri]
The word *geography* has four syllables:	*ge | og | ra | phy*	[dʒi|ɒg|rə|fi]

Fill in this chart using the words in the vocabulary list on page 44.

One-Syllable Words	Two-Syllable Words	Words with Three or More Syllables*
star	descríbe	rádius
soil	revólve	gálaxy
live	consíst	áverage
cold	áxis	cóntinent
land	plánet	diámeter
hot	rótate	úniverse
big turn	dístance	
freeze close	compáre	
far small		
large		
grow		

*When you pronounce a longer word, not all the syllables get the same stress, or force. The dictionary shows stress with a mark ('). With the help of a dictionary, compare the pronunciation of the words *geography* [dʒi'ɒgrəfi] and *geographic* [dʒiə'græfɪk].

46 · Earthbound

I. The Sun's Family

A. Fill in the blanks with the words provided. Use each word only once.

radius   gas   soil   star   rocks

planets   freezes   revolve   rotate

1. The Sun is a __star__.

2. The Sun's solar system includes nine __planets__.

3. All planets __rotate__, or turn, on their axes.

4. The earth and eight other planets __revolve__ around the Sun.

5. When you double the __radius__ of a circle, you get its diameter.

6. When water reaches 0°C, it __freezes__.

7. The Rocky Mountains in North America have their name because they are full of __rocks__.

8. Trees and plants grow in __soil__.

9. Air is not a liquid but a __gas__.

B. Look at the following chart about the planets in the solar system.

1. What kind of information about the planets do we need to fill in the blank fields?

The Earth and Its Neighbors · 47

2. Scan the dictionary entries on p. 48 and fill in the missing information in the chart.

Planet in the Solar System	Diameter	Distance from the Sun
Mercury	3000	36.2 mil. miles
Pluto	1400	2.8–4.6 billion miles
Mars	4218	141.6 mil. miles
Venus	7600	67.2 mil. miles
Earth	7,900 miles	92.96 mil. miles
Neptune	28,000	2.8 billion miles
Uranus	30,000	1,790,000,000
Saturn	74,000	886,000,000
Jupiter	86,000	483 mil. miles

Earth /ɜrθ/ n. It is the third planet from the Sun. The earth takes 365.26 days to revolve around the Sun. Its distance from the Sun is about 92.96 million miles. The average radius of the earth is 3,959 miles. As far as we know today, the earth is the only planet with enough air and water to support life.

Jupiter /dʒu:pətər/ n. It is the fifth planet from the Sun. Jupiter is the largest planet in the solar system. But it only has a rocky core and 99 percent of this planet is gas. It has a diameter of approximately 86,000 miles. It is about 318 times bigger than the earth. The average distance of this planet from the Sun is about 483 million miles.

Mars /mɑrz/ n. It is the fourth planet from the Sun. Mars takes about 687 days to revolve around the Sun. The average distance to the Sun is 141.6 million miles. The temperature on this planet is always below freezing. The mean radius of this planet is approximately 2,090 miles. Mars is also called the Red Planet because the soil is red and the sky on Mars looks orange.

Mercury /mɜ:kjʊri/ n. It is closer to the Sun than all the other planets. This planet is hot, dry, and airless. One day on Mercury is about 88 Earth days long. At "noon," the temperature on Mercury is 800°F. At "night," the temperature is -300°F. The mean distance between Mercury and the Sun is 36.2 million miles. The mean radius of this planet is approximately 1,500 miles.

Neptune /neptu:n/ n. It is the eighth planet from the Sun. Neptune has a mean distance from the Sun of 2.8 billion miles. The mean radius of this planet is 14,000 miles. This planet always has very strong winds. Neptune has four thin rings and eight moons around it.

Pluto /plu:təʊ/ n. It is smaller than all planets in the solar system. It is also farther from the Sun than all other planets. Pluto takes about 248.4 years to revolve around the Sun. It is between 2.8 and 4.6 billion miles away from the Sun. Therefore, this planet is very cold and probably consists of ice. Its diameter is approximately 1,400 miles.

Saturn /sætərn/ n. It is the sixth planet from the Sun. On pictures of Saturn you can see thousands of rings around it. Saturn has a diameter of 74,000 miles. It is nine times larger than Earth. Its distance from the Sun is 886,000,000 miles.

Uranus /jʊrənəs/ n. This is the seventh planet from the Sun. It takes 84.02 years to revolve around the Sun. Uranus is about 1,790,000,000 miles away from the Sun. It has a diameter of 30,000 miles. On pictures you can see that Uranus is not standing upright. This planet is on its side, turned almost 90°.

Venus /vi:nəs/ n. It is the second planet from the Sun. Its average radius is 3,800 miles. It almost has the same size as the earth (the earth is 7,900 miles in diameter). Venus is hotter than all other planets in the solar system. Its temperature is 900°F. Because of this heat, there is no water on this planet. Its average distance from the Sun is about 67.2 million miles. One night on Venus lasts four Earth months because the planet turns very slowly.

The Earth and Its Neighbors · 49

C. Look at the picture of the planets that is on the first page of this chapter or the chart in Activity B. Then fill in the missing names of the planets in the following sentences.

1. _Jupiter_ is *larger* than Saturn.

2. _Pluto_ is *smaller* than Mercury.

3. _Mercury_ is *closer* to the Sun than Venus.

4. _Pluto_ is sometimes *farther* from the Sun than Neptune. c.f. p.47

D. Go back to the sentences in Activity C and look at the words *larger, smaller, closer,* and *farther.* Do you know what part of speech they are?

Comparison

Words like *small* or *large* are called *adjectives.* An adjective describes a noun or a person. When adjectives are used to compare two nouns, they are called *comparative adjectives.*

Use the comparative form of adjectives to compare two objects, people, or places.
Use the word *than* after the comparative form of the adjective and before the object you are comparing.

   Mars is *smaller than* the earth.
   Uranus is *bigger than* Neptune.

Write more sentences about the planets. Use the words *smaller, bigger, farther from, closer to.* Follow the examples in the language box "Comparison."

_____

_____

_____

50 · Earthbound

_____

_____
_____
_____

E. When an adjective is used in a comparison, it changes its form. Not all comparative adjectives are formed the same way. Study the information in the next language box and then fill in the blanks with the correct form of the adjective.

Formation of Comparative Adjectives

1. To make the comparative form of a *one-syllable adjective -er* is usually added to the base form.

    small → small**er**   warm → warm**er**

2. When the *word ends in a vowel + consonant* (i.e., -ot or -ig) double the last consonant and add *-er*.

    big → bi**gg**er   hot → ho**tt**er

3. For other words with *more than one syllable* add the word *more* before the adjective and don't change the base form.

    in terest ing → *more* interesting   fa mous → *more* famous

    prettier ?
4. The adjectives *good, bad,* and *far* have *irregular* comparative forms.

    good → *better*   bad → *worse*   far → *farther*

(margin note: General rules)

1. Pluto is _____ (small) than most of the other planets.

2. The Sun is _____ (hot) than Planet Earth.

3. Planet Earth is _____ (interesting) than other planets because many people live on this planet.

4. The living conditions for animals, plants, and human beings are _____ (good) on Earth than on Venus.

5. The living conditions on Mercury are probably _____ (bad) than on Venus because it is closer to the Sun.

6. Jupiter is _____ (warm) than Pluto because it is closer to the Sun.

7. The Moon is _____ (famous) than most of the planets in the solar system because people have visited the Moon.

8. Neptune is _____ (far) from the Sun than Uranus.

9. Jupiter is _____ (big) than Saturn.

F. You are going to read a passage. Before you start reading, look at the title of the reading passage and at the picture at the beginning of this chapter. Then answer the following questions on a separate sheet of paper.

write on board - ?'s + "The Sun's Family. Have Ss look at p. 43

1. What will the passage probably be about? *planets close to sun*
2. What does the word *family* mean here? *things that belong together*
3. Close your book and write down five words that will probably be in the text. *star, planet, earth, big, far*

Previewing

The skill you have just used is called *previewing*. When we talked about maps, we said that we look at a map to find out where we need to go. We do the same thing before we start reading. We look at all the information we can get (titles, pictures) and think about it before we start the journey through the text. This helps us to remember and understand what the text is about.

THE SUN'S FAMILY

1   The Sun is a star. It is a huge ball of glowing gases. It provides
2   heat and light. Nine planets revolve around the Sun. Earth is one of

them. The other eight planets are Mercury, Venus, Mars, Jupiter, Saturn, Uranus, Neptune, and Pluto. Each planet has its own path around the Sun. This path around the Sun is called the planet's orbit. The family of planets and the moons and other objects that also revolve around the Sun are called the solar system. Some people also call it the Sun's family.

Two of the planets—Mercury and Venus—are closer to the Sun than Earth is. Because they are closer, they have very hot temperatures. They are so hot—more than 800°F—that life probably cannot exist on them. The other planets are farther from the Sun than Earth is. For this reason, they are also a lot colder. From what we know now, there seems to be no water or warmth to support life on these planets. Earth, as far as we know, is the only planet revolving around the Sun that supports life. It has temperatures that are not too hot and not too cold. There is also enough water for plants, animals, and people to live on the earth.

Planet Earth is only one very small part of the solar system. However, the solar system is just one very small part of a larger family of stars. These stars make up our galaxy. The name of our galaxy is the Milky Way. There may be 100 billion stars in the Milky Way. Scientists today are not sure, but probably each star also has a solar system around it.

Our galaxy is called the Milky Way because it looks as if someone spilled a pail of milk across the sky. If you look up into the sky on a very clear night, you can see part of the Milky Way. It is a very bright band of light going from north to south across the sky.

Far, far out beyond our galaxy are billions of other galaxies. Together, all the galaxies make up the universe. The universe includes the earth and the rest of our solar system, all the stars, and the galaxies.

G. Choose the correct form of the verb or adjective. Circle the letter of the answer that you have chosen. Write Adj. (for adjective) or V (for verb) next to your answer.

1. Mercury and Venus _____ two planets.

    a. was
    b. are
    c. is

2. The Earth _____ around the Sun.

   a. revolves
   b. rotates
   c. revolve

3. Each planet _____ its own orbit.

   a. have
   b. had
   c. has

4. Mercury and Venus are _____ to the Sun than the earth is.

   a. more close
   b. closest
   c. closer

5. Pluto is _____ away from the Sun than Saturn.

   a. farther
   b. farthest
   c. more far

6. The solar system is one small part in a _____ family of stars.

   a. largest
   b. more larger
   c. larger

H. For each group of words, cross out the term that does not belong there. If you are not sure, go back to the text "The Sun's Family" and scan for the information. When you find the term, write on the blank line underneath the words why it does not belong to the group.

Example:

Uranus   Neptune   Pluto   ~~the Sun~~

Uranus, Neptune, and Pluto are planets. The Sun is a star.

54 · Earthbound

1. Venus   ~~solar system~~   Mars   Mercury

2. Jupiter   Saturn   ~~Venus~~   Uranus
   V is hot, others are cold

3. ~~Earth~~   Pluto   Jupiter   Saturn
   only people live on Earth

4. star   planet   the Moon   ~~Milky Way~~
   Includes the others

5. stars   planets   galaxies   ~~universe~~
   includes others

I. Here are two groups of words consisting of general and specific terms. Put the words in a numerical order (1, 2, 3, . . .) that shows which words are more general and which are more specific. Begin with number 1 for the most general word.

general	1	2	3	4	5	6	specific

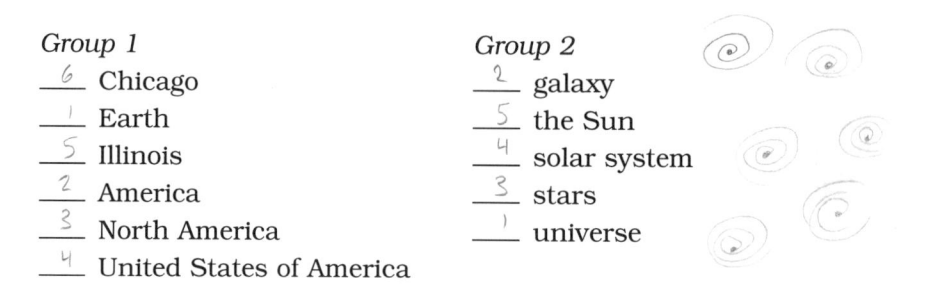

Group 1
_6_ Chicago
_1_ Earth
_5_ Illinois
_2_ America
_3_ North America
_4_ United States of America

Group 2
_2_ galaxy
_5_ the Sun
_4_ solar system
_3_ stars
_1_ universe

J. Now create your own group of words and let your classmates guess the most general word that describes this group of words. Follow these steps.

1. Think of one general word that includes other more specific words.
2. Write the more specific words underneath the general word you already have.

The Earth and Its Neighbors · 55

3. Read the word list to your classmates and ask them to tell you the general word you were thinking of.

Examples:

a. ocean   lake   pond   b. planets   stars   galaxies
General Word: bodies of water   General Word: universe

General word: _____

II. Discovering Planet Earth

A. Today, Alexander von Humboldt is a famous man because he studied Planet Earth long before the field of geography even existed. Before you read the passage about his life and work, think about the following questions.

1. When do you think von Humboldt lived?
2. What did he probably like to do?
3. Why do you think he became famous?

Painting of Alexander von Humboldt by Friedrich Georg Weitsch.

B. Read the story about Alexander von Humboldt.

THE STORY OF ALEXANDER VON HUMBOLDT

1   Geography is a very old science. Several hundred years ago,
2 some scientists thought that their main goal was to describe the
3 world and develop maps of the earth. People all over the world

wanted to learn more about the places where they lived and about other countries. One person who was interested in nature and lands more than 200 years ago was Alexander von Humboldt. Von Humboldt was one of the important scientists at the time. He traveled all over the world and recorded what he saw. Today, many people think that he is the founder of modern geography.

Alexander von Humboldt was born in 1769 in Berlin, Germany. When he was young he was not interested in science. However, he was interested in nature and different cultures. It was his dream to travel and learn about the earth.

At first, he only traveled in Europe. At the beginning of the nineteenth century he went to Central and South America. During his travels, von Humboldt recorded all the information he could get. So when he came back from his trips he always brought many maps, diagrams, and charts back to Europe. After he had completed his last journey, he spent his last 25 years writing 30 volumes on what he found in America. Von Humboldt died in 1859.

Alexander von Humboldt's observations and descriptions started a new way of looking at the earth. His studies were different from the studies of other scientists at the time. Others only observed and described, but von Humboldt also measured and compared. He measured the land, air, and plants in certain areas, put them into groups according to similarity, and compared them with what he found in other areas of the world. In addition, he investigated cause-effect relationships. In other words, he not only described what happened, he also tried to explain why it happened. For example, he gave the first description of the relation between altitude, air temperature, vegetation, and agriculture in tropical mountains. This kind of approach is common in geography today.

Adapted from *World Geography—People and Places* (Mission Hills, CA: Glencoe/McGraw Hill, 1989).

C. Are the following statements about the reading passage true or false? For each statement write true (T) or false (F) in the answer blanks.

  9 1. Another name for Alexander von Humboldt is "founder of modern geography." _T_
 10 2. Alexander von Humboldt was born in Europe. _T_
12-13 3. Von Humboldt did not like to travel. _F_
 19 4. Von Humboldt spent 25 years of his life writing books. _T_
 20 5. The geographer Alexander von Humboldt died in 1895. _F_

24-25 6. His books were different because he measured and compared what he saw in different countries. __T__

32 7. Modern geographers study cause-effect relationships. __T__

D. Add important events in Alexander von Humboldt's life to the time line.

1769	*Travels in Europe*	1800 *Travels in C.A. & S.A.*	1834 *started writing*	1859 *died*
(born in Berlin)				

E. Alexander von Humboldt lived in the eighteenth and nineteenth centuries. Therefore, most of the story about von Humboldt is written in the past tense. Read the story a second time and circle ten verbs. (Do not circle any form of the verb *be*.) You will probably find many verbs that are used in their past tense form.

58 · **Earthbound**

Simple Past Tense

The *simple past tense* is used to talk about activities or situations that began and ended in the past. English has regular and irregular verbs. They form the past tense in different ways.

Formation of Simple Past Tense

Regular verbs form the simple past tense with *-ed*. The spelling of regular verbs changes when the final letter is a *-y*.

> Geographers *answer* questions today. *(present tense)*
> Geographers *answered* questions 200 years ago. *(past tense)*

> I *study* geography this semester. *(present tense)*
> I *studied* geography last year. *(past tense)*

For *irregular verbs* the spelling is different. You have to memorize the spelling for each word.

> Geographers *think* about the earth. *(present tense)*
> Geographers *thought* about the earth. *(past tense)*

In negative sentences and questions you use the *past tense of do (= did)* + verb.

> *Do* you *study* geography this semester? *(present tense)*
> *Did* you *study* geography last semester? *(past tense)*

> I *don't study* geography this semester. *(present tense)*
> I *didn't study* geography last semester. *(past tense)*

F. Do you know the past tense form of the words given in the following list? Find them in the story about von Humboldt and write them down. Also write down the subjects of the sentences that contain these verbs.

Present Tense   *Past Tense*

think   scientists *thought*

live   _____

travel _____

record _____

go _____

come _____

bring _____

spend _____

find _____

die _____

start _____

observe and describe _____

measure and compare _____

investigate _____

put _____

compare _____

try _____

give _____

G. Explain why these two sentences in the text about von Humboldt are in simple present tense and not in past tense.
1. Geography is a very old science. (line 1) *express general/timeless truth*
2. Today, many people think that he is the founder of modern geography. (lines 8/9) *① Present tense expresses action, event taking place in present – ② "Today..."*

60 · Earthbound

Rule: 1. <u>actions, events in present</u>

2. <u>Today - indicates time frame</u>

H. Can you find another sentence in the von Humboldt story that was written in the present tense? Explain why the verb is not used in the past tense.

line 12 - This kind of approach is common in geography today.

I. On the time line write important events in your own life. Then write a short description about yourself using the past tense. Begin the story with the date you were born.

Chapter 4

The Earth in Stories

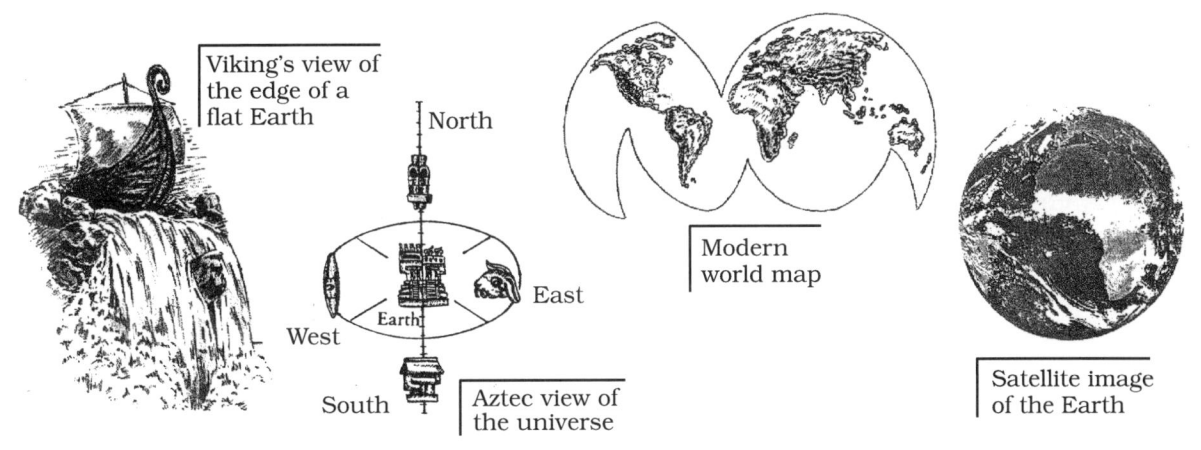

Viking's view of the edge of a flat Earth

Aztec view of the universe

Modern world map

Satellite image of the Earth

Adapted from *Visual Factfinder: Planet Earth* by Neil Curtis and Michael Allaby, copyright © Grisewood & Dempsey Ltd. 1993. Reprinted with permission of Larousse Kingfisher Chambers Inc., New York.

A Look Behind/A Look Ahead

In the previous chapter, you learned about the solar system and about the fact that geographers have always tried to observe and explain what they found on the earth. But long before famous geographers traveled around the world, people already had an interest in explaining what they saw and felt in their world. Some of these ancient ideas about the earth were confirmed in modern science, but most of them only continue to exist as myths, or old stories. In this chapter we will go on a journey through the ancient world of storytelling. The chapter will show that different people had different ideas about the earth and its formation. You will hear about some stories that people in ancient times told about the earth. Most of the time people's ideas were influenced by their style of living or their religion.

To the Student

At the end of this chapter, you will be able to

1. tell an old Native American story about the creation of the earth;
2. describe different theories and ideas about the earth;
3. understand what people's ideas about the earth were based on.

Vocabulary Development

Read the following list of important words from chapter 4 (you may have seen some of them in previous chapters). If you already know the word, put a check mark (✓) in the space in front of the word. When you finish the chapter, return to this list. Mark all the new words you learned. Write down additional words that you learned. (The words that are italicized here will be used in an exercise that appears later in the chapter.)

__ earthquake	__ symbol	__ myth	__ description
__ animal	__ religion	__ creation	__ world
__ culture	__ plant	__ roots	__ seeds
__ compass	__ hole	__ skin	__ *explain*
__ *believe*	__ *represent*	__ rest	__ *spend*
__ *include*	__ *move*	__ *invent*	__ dream
__ *fail*	__ *develop*	__ *float*	__ hold up
__ be successful	__ flat	__ under	__ above
__ strong	__ different	__ hollow	__ tiny

_____	_____	_____	_____
_____	_____	_____	_____
_____	_____	_____	_____
_____	_____	_____	_____

The pronunciation focus for this chapter is the regular past tense. The regular past tense has *three pronunciations.* Most verbs add the consonant [d] (for voiced sounds) or [t] (for voiceless sounds).

[t] as in liked
[d] as in robbed

Verbs already ending in [t] or [d] add an extra syllable: [ɪd] or [əd] as in visited or landed.

Listen especially for these sounds when you practice new words with your classmates and teacher. Look at the vocabulary list and find the italicized verbs. Each of these verbs has one of the four sounds in the past tense form. One of these verbs has two different past tense forms. Can you guess which one it is? Write the past tense form of these words in the correct position in the chart that follows. When you are done with the chapter, try to add more words to this list.

[t]	[d]	[ɪd]/[əd]

I. The Earth on Turtle's Back

A. In ancient days, different people had different ideas about the shape of the earth and its formation. Like many other people on the earth, the Native Americans passed on these ideas by telling stories to their children. Therefore, these stories were passed down orally from one generation to the next. One example of such a story is "The Earth on Turtle's Back." It is a tale that was told by the Oneida tribe of Native Americans. These people are part of the Iroquois League and used to live in what today is called New York and Delaware. This tale talks about many different animals. Look at the pictures of these animals and then answer the questions about them by filling in the appropriate animal name in each of the following sentences.

a duck

a swan

a loon

a muskrat

a turtle

a beaver

1. A _____ looks like a big rat, but it has thicker fur and can live on land and in the water.

2. Everybody thinks that a _____ walks very slowly. This animal is, however, a swift swimmer.

3. Both the _____, _____, and the _____ have webbed feet. They need these special feet with the skin between the toes because they spend time in the water and swim a lot.

4. A _____ is a very strong and swift animal that lives in the water and uses wood pieces or roots to build houses in the water.

5. A _____ cannot float on its back, but a _____ can.

6. Human beings have hunted the _____ for its shell and its meat.

7. When a _____ spreads out its wings, it looks very big.

8. The _____ has very short legs. This water bird can swim well, but it is not a very good diver.

B. Listen to the story and read along.

The Earth on Turtle's Back

1 Before this earth existed, there was only water. As far as one
2 could see, there was only water. In that water there were birds and
3 animals swimming around. Far above the water, there was *Skyland*.
4 In Skyland there was a very big and beautiful tree. It had four white
5 roots, and from its branches all kinds of different fruits and flowers
6 grew.
7 There was also an ancient chief in Skyland. He lived there with
8 his young wife, who was expecting a child. One night she dreamed
9 that she saw the great tree uprooted. She told her husband about
10 the dream, and he said that it was a very powerful dream. Such a
11 powerful dream, he thought, must come true. He wanted the tree to
12 be uprooted.
13 The ancient chief asked the young men to pull up the tree, but
14 the roots were so deep that they could not do it. He himself then

came to the tree and wrapped his arms around it, bent his knees, and pulled. Finally, he was able to uproot the tree and place it on its side. Where the tree's roots used to be there was now a big hole. The chief's wife leaned over to look down. She held onto one of the tree's branches and leaned out further to see what was in the hole. But then, she lost her balance. She fell into the deep, deep hole. In her hand she had seeds of the big and beautiful tree.

Far, far below in the waters, some of the birds and animals looked up. "Someone is falling toward us from the sky," said one of the birds. "We must do something to help her," said another. Then two swans flew up. They caught the woman between their wide wings and slowly began to bring her down as all the other animals were watching.

"She is not like us," said one of the animals. "Look she doesn't have webbed feet. I don't think she can live in the water." "What shall we do then?" said another of the water animals. "I know," said one of the water birds. "I have heard that there is earth far below the waters. If we dive down and bring up earth, then she will have a place to stand." So the animals decided that they had to help. One after another tried to bring up earth.

Some say the duck dove down first. He swam down and down, far beneath the surface, but he could not reach the bottom and floated back up. Then the beaver tried. The beaver went even deeper, so that it was all dark, but he could not reach the bottom either. Next, the loon, who had very strong wings, tried. Although the loon was gone a long time, he failed too. Soon it seemed that all had tried and all had failed. Then a small voice spoke, "I will bring up earth or die trying."

They looked to see who it was. It was the tiny muskrat. She dove down and swam and swam. She was not as strong or as swift as the others, but she was determined. She went so deep that it was all dark, and still she swam deeper. At last, just as she was becoming unconscious, she reached out one small paw and grasped at the bottom of the sea. The tiny muskrat barely touched the ground before she floated up, almost dead.

When the other animals saw her come to the surface they thought she had failed. Then they saw her right paw was held tightly shut. "She has the earth," they said. "Now where can we put it?" "Place it on my back," said a deep voice. It was the great turtle.

They brought the muskrat over to the great turtle and placed her paw against the turtle's back. To this day there are marks at the back of the turtle's shell which were made by the muskrat's paw. The tiny bit of earth fell on the back of the turtle. Almost immediately, it began to grow larger and larger and larger until it became the whole world.

Then the two swans brought the sky woman down. She stepped onto the new earth and opened her hand. All the seeds that she had in her hand fell onto the bare soil. From those seeds the trees and the grass grew up. Life on Earth had begun.

(From *Keepers of the Earth: Native American Stories and Environmental Activities for Children* © 1988 by Michael J. Caduto and Joseph Bruchac. With permission of the publisher, Fulcrum Publishing, Inc. Golden, Colorado 80401 [800] 992-2908.)

C. Read each sentence and then circle a, b, or c to complete the sentence according to the story "The Earth on Turtle's Back."

1. The leader of a Native American tribe is called a ____a____.

    a. chief
    b. king
    c. president

2. In the story "The Earth on Turtle's Back," the chief asks the other men to ____b____ the tree.

    a. uprooted
    b. uproot
    c. roots

3. When the chief's wife wanted to look at the hole in the sky, she could not see much at first. Then she ____a____ to see better.

    a. leaned over
    b. leaned backward
    c. leaned against

4. The chief's wife lost her ____b____ and fell through the hole in the sky.

    a. branches
    b. balance
    c. seeds

68 · Earthbound

5. The muskrat brought up the earth. She was the only animal that did not ___c___.

   a. failure
   b. failed
   c. fail

6. The story "The Earth on Turtle's Back" shows that ___a___ is important if one wants to achieve a goal.

   a. determination
   b. determined
   c. determine

7. The muskrat held her breath for so long that she almost became ___a___.

   a. unconscious
   b. conscious
   c. unconsciously

8. When the muskrat reached the bottom of the sea, she ___a___ the ground.

   a. grasped at
   b. grasped in
   c. grasped on

9. The muskrat was successful and brought up some ___a___ from the bottom of the sea.

   a. soil
   b. floor
   c. land

10. When the muskrat put the earth on the turtle's back, there were no plants on it. It was ___a___.

    a. bare
    b. soiled
    c. seeds

The Earth in Stories · 69

D. Look at this series of pictures. They show the story "The Earth on Turtle's Back." Put the pictures in the correct order by writing a number to the left of each one. Then tell the story using your own words.

a. 3

b. 4

c. 1

d. 6

70 · Earthbound

e

2

f

5

E. Are the following statements about the story true or false? Write true (T) or false (F) in the first answer blank for each statement. Then write in the second answer blank where you found the information (which line or lines in the story).

1. The Oneida tribe believed that in the beginning there was no water on the earth. F

    line(s) ___1___

2. The trees in Skyland were very different from our trees today. T

    line(s) ___4___

3. The chief's wife was pregnant. T

    line(s) ___8___

4. The chief was not paying attention to what his wife was telling him. F

    line(s) ___10___

The Earth in Stories · 71

5. The young men in Skyland pulled the tree out of the ground. _F_

    line(s) ___14___

6. The chief's wife wanted to fall down from the sky. _F_

    line(s) ___20___

7. Two swans caught the chief's wife when she fell down from Skyland. _T_

    line(s) ___25___

8. The animals were very surprised to see the woman. _T_

    line(s) ___28___

9. The animals brought up the earth because the chief told them to do so. _F_

    line(s) ___31-2___

10. The great turtle was able to bring up the earth from the bottom of the sea. _F_

    line(s) ___51___

11. The muskrat scratched the back of the turtle's shell. _T_

    line(s) ___55___

12. The chief's wife brought seeds from Skyland to the earth. _T_

    line(s) ___21, 61___

72 · **Earthbound**

F. With a partner, discuss why the tiny muskrat and not the strong loon brought up the earth from the bottom of the sea. Does the story told by the Oneida tribe have a moral? That means, is there another reason (besides describing the creation of the earth) to tell this story to other people?

G. Look at the story "The Earth on Turtle's Back" again. The story is divided into paragraphs. In English, texts are usually divided into paragraphs. Paragraphs make reading easier because they tell the reader what belongs together.

Paragraphs

1. A paragraph is a group of sentences related to a single topic (subject). In a longer text the paragraphs are related to each other, but each paragraph only has one idea.
2. A paragraph begins with an indented line, so that you can see where a new paragraph begins.
3. A paragraph usually (but not always) has a topic sentence or main idea that tells the reader what the paragraph is about.

How many paragraphs does the story "The Earth on Turtle's Back" have? _____

H. Each paragraph in a story has one idea. For the first three paragraphs in the story "The Earth on Turtle's Back," circle the letter of the sentence that best describes the idea of the whole paragraph.

Paragraph 1
   a. This paragraph describes the birds and animals in Skyland.
   (b.) This paragraph describes what everything looked like before the earth existed.
   c. This paragraph describes a big and beautiful tree in Skyland.

Paragraph 2
   (a.) This paragraph explains why a tree in Skyland was uprooted.
   b. This paragraph is about a very important dream in Skyland.
   c. This paragraph is about the chief of Skyland and his wife's baby.

Paragraph 3
a. This paragraph describes how strong the chief of Skyland was.
b. This paragraph explains how the tree was uprooted.
(c.) This paragraph describes how and why the chief's wife fell down from the sky.

I. You have looked at the first three paragraphs of the story "The Earth on Turtle's Back." Each of the following ideas describes one of the remaining paragraphs. Go back to the text and match the sentences with the paragraph they are describing. Write the number of the paragraph on the line following the sentence. The first one has been done for you.

1. why the turtle, even today, has marks on her back (Paragraph _9_)
2. how the swans caught the woman (Paragraph _4_)
3. why we have plants and life on the earth (Paragraph _10_)
4. how the animals were discussing what they should do (Paragraph _5_)
5. when the great turtle offers her help (Paragraph _8_)
6. how the duck, the beaver, and the loon tried to bring up the earth from the bottom of the sea (Paragraph _6_)
7. how the muskrat brought up the earth from the bottom of the sea (Paragraph _7_)

II. Different Ideas about the Earth

A. Fill in the blanks with the following words.

believe	hollow	goddess
holds	represented	rested

1. People from different cultures often have different religions and _____ in different gods.

2. Some cultures believed that the earth _____ on a huge animal.

74 · Earthbound

3. A mountain usually consists of solid rock. It is not _____.

4. Gravity _____ up all the objects and living creatures on the earth.

5. In many different cultures people believed that certain animals _____ a god.

6. A female god is called a _____.

B. People have always tried to explain what the world looks like. Many times their ideas were influenced by their religion. Following are three different descriptions from different time periods and different areas of the world. Fill in the blanks with the correct past tense form of the verb.

1. The Babylonians, who _____ (live) around 3000 B.C., _____ (have) their own idea about the earth. They _____ (believe) that the earth _____ (is) a hollow mountain. They also _____ (believe) that the sea _____ (is) under and around this mountain. Inside this mountain they _____ (think) was the dark world of the dead. Across the curve of the sky _____ (move) the Sun, the Moon, and the stars.

2. Egyptians _____ (explain) the world with the help of their gods. Therefore, they _____ (see) the earth as a resting god. They also _____ (see) the heavens as a gracefully bent goddess above the god. The space between these two _____ (is) occupied by the god of atmosphere. This god _____ (sup-

port) the skies or, in other words, this god was holding up the sky. The Sun god, who was sitting in a boat, _____ (sail) each day across the heavens into the death of night.

3. Hindus in India _____ (have) many ideas about the earth. Some _____ (think) that eight giant elephants _____ (hold up), or supported, the earth. They _____ (think) that when the elephants _____ (move), there would be an earthquake. The elephants _____ (stand) on a turtle. This turtle _____ (represent) the god Vishnu. It _____ (rest) on a cobra. The cobra _____ (is) very important in the picture because it _____ (is) the symbol for water and nobody can live on Earth without water.

Text adapted from Arthur Beiser, *The Earth* (Alexandria, VA: Time Life Books, 1970).

C. Match the pictures with the corresponding paragraphs in Activity B.

a

b

76 · **Earthbound**

c

D. Go back to Activity B. In each paragraph, circle the name of the people that the paragraph talks about and answer the following questions.

1. Where did you find this information, at the beginning or the end of the description?

2. Why do you think the information appears in this position in the text?

Topic Sentence

English speakers think that each description in Activity B forms a *paragraph*. A *paragraph* is a group of sentences about one topic. When you read the paragraphs in Activity B again, you will see that they all include a sentence that gives the topic of the entire paragraph. This type of sentence is called the *topic sentence* of the paragraph. The *topic sentence* helps you read and understand the whole paragraph. The topic sentence is usually, but not always, the first sentence of a paragraph. It is always the most general sentence in a paragraph.

The Earth in Stories · 77

   3. Underline the topic sentence in each description in Activity B.

E. Look at the two pictures (*a* and *b*) and read the sentences. Then decide which sentences belong to which picture (four sentences in each description). Write the sentences for picture *a* on the blank lines under the *a* heading on p. 79. Write the sentences for picture *b* under the *b* heading on p. 79.

a

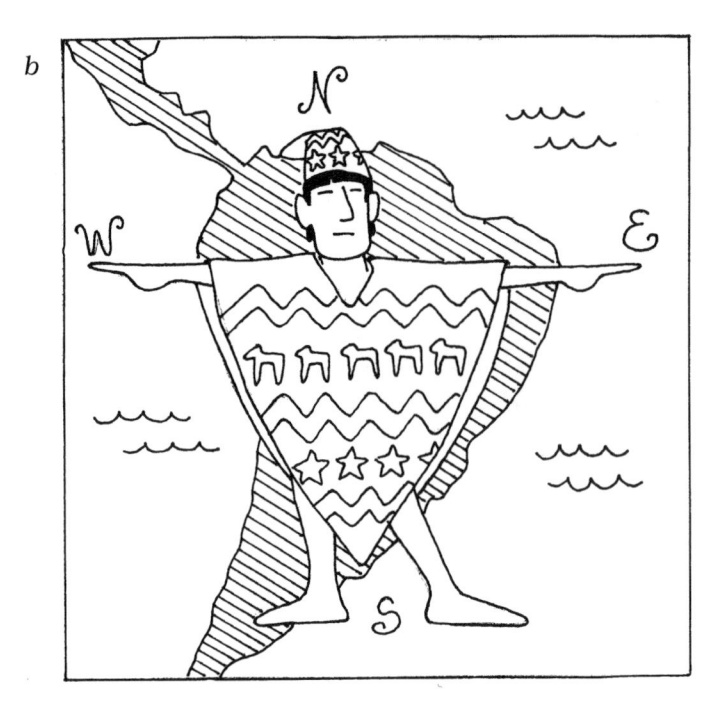

1. They thought that when you sailed to the end of the ocean, you would just fall down and disappear forever.
2. The Vikings, who lived in Europe 1,000 years ago, believed that the earth was flat.
3. The Aztecs lived in America before Cortés invaded the country in 1519.
4. Therefore, they were able to include the four points of the compass in their description of the world.
5. In fact, they not only believed that it was flat, they also thought that the land and the ocean had an end.
6. Their culture was very well developed, and the Aztecs knew a lot about the sciences and especially about the earth.
7. Since the Vikings spent much of their time in boats on the water, these ideas about the ocean were very important in their culture.
8. In fact, they thought that the earth was in the middle of north, south, east, and west.

a

1. _____

2. _____

3. _____

4. _____

b

1. _____

2. _____

3. _____

4. _____

F. Go back to Activity E and find the most general sentence, or topic sentence, for each description. Write the two sentences on a separate piece of paper. Then complete each paragraph using the remaining sentences in the correct order. To help you find the correct order, study the language box first.

> *Cohesive Devices*
>
> Words that help readers understand the structure of a text are called *cohesive devices*. Some cohesive devices are used in texts because writers don't want to repeat the same word over and over again. Pronouns often function as such cohesive devices.
>
> Another important type of cohesive device is *logical connectors*. They describe the relationship between two independent sentences.
>
> *Pronouns*
>
> > *Alexander von Humboldt* was a famous geographer. *He* studied the Earth.
> > (The personal pronoun *he* replaces the name in the second sentence.)
> > *This man* liked to measure and compare the things he found on Earth.
> > (The demonstrative pronoun *this* + the word *man* replaces the name.)
>
> *Logical Connectors*
>
> > Mercury is the planet nearest to the Sun. *Therefore*, it is very hot.
> > (The second sentence gives the result of the first sentence.)
> > The Earth provides air and water for living creatures. *In fact*, it is the only planet in the solar system that can support life.
> > (The second sentence gives additional information.)

G. Go back to Activity B and find all the pronouns that occur at the beginning of a sentence. Then draw an arrow from each pronoun to the word it refers to.

H. Find a partner for this activity. One member of your group looks at the picture of the Viking in Activity E. The other person looks at the picture here. This picture is a copy of the picture in Activity E, but some things have been changed. Describe your picture to your partner and try to find the differences without looking at both pictures.

The Earth in Stories · **81**

I. The following paragraphs talk about myths. Select an appropriate topic sentence (a, b, or c) for each of the paragraphs and write it on the blank line.

Paragraph 1

_____

_____

In those days natural events, like thunder or earthquakes, often seemed strange and fantastic to the people. Telling stories about these events helped the people to live with nature and not to be scared. These stories, or myths, became an important part of daily life. In some way they explained what people saw or experienced. In many parts of the world, myths were passed on orally from one generation to the next, and since they explained natural events, people were not so scared anymore.

    a. In ancient times storytelling played a special role in society.
    b. Myths show that people are scared of fantastic events in nature.
    c. Myths that explain fantastic events are usually not written down.

82 · Earthbound

Paragraph 2

_____

_____

The ancient Greeks, for example, believed that the god Atlas held the earth on his shoulders. The Mongolians, on the other hand, thought that a gigantic frog held the weight of the earth. Each time one of these figures stumbled under the great weight, the ground shook with an earthquake.

a. In Greek mythology Atlas was a huge creature who held up the earth.
b. Many cultures believed that the earth was held up by a huge creature.
c. Earthquakes always happen when a huge creature stumbles on a stone.

Paragraph 3

_____

_____

A Japanese myth, for example, says that earthquakes are caused by a giant catfish. Normally the gods keep the catfish under control by holding it down with a large rock. But during October, when the gods are away, the fish may get loose and cause a lot of damage. The myth also says that earthquakes occur because the gods are angry and they want to punish the people with a volcano eruption or an earthquake.

a. In Japan angry gods often punish the people with a dangerous volcano eruption.
b. According to a Japanese myth, giant catfish are huge fish that the gods keep under some large rocks.
c. People on the earth have always tried to explain natural events like storms or earthquakes.

J. Do you know an interesting story or myth about your country, the shape of the world, or the world's creation? Write it down and ask a partner to read it or tell him or her your story. Has your partner ever heard about this story? (If you cannot remember a story, try to invent one.)

Chapter 5

The Earth in Motion

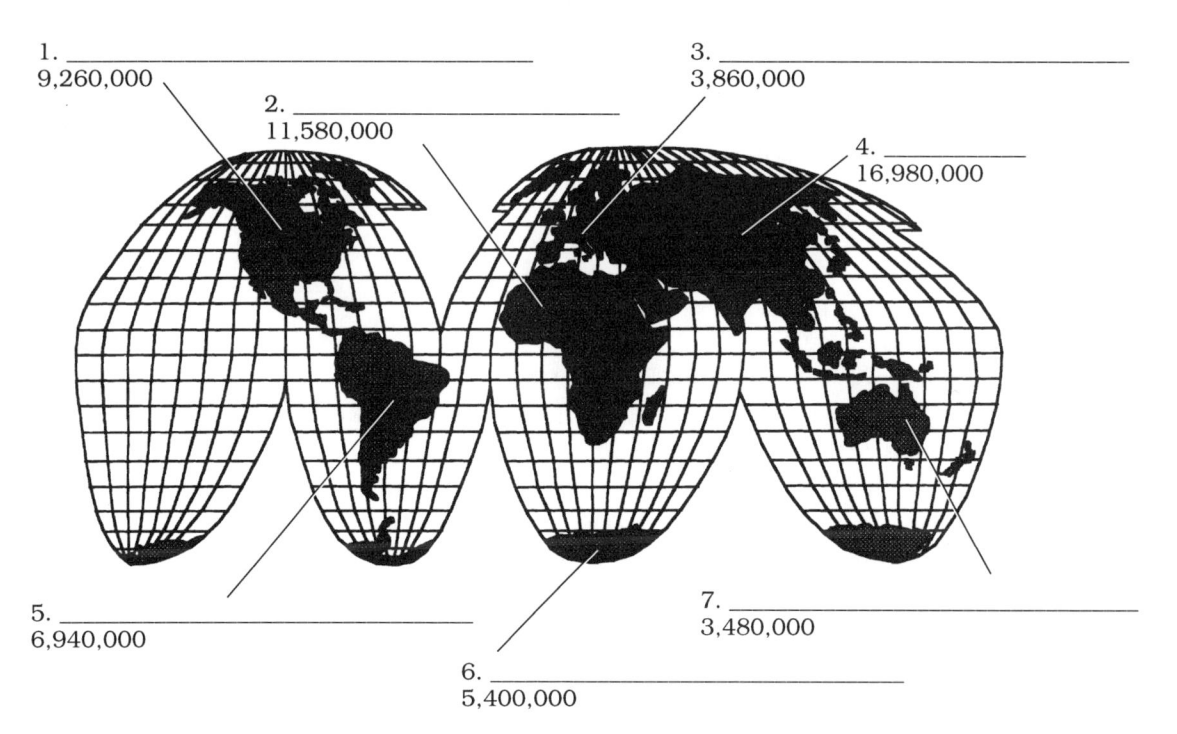

1. _____
9,260,000

2. _____
11,580,000

3. _____
3,860,000

4. _____
16,980,000

5. _____
6,940,000

6. _____
5,400,000

7. _____
3,480,000

Write down the name of each continent on the blank line above the square miles.

A Look Behind/A Look Ahead

The last chapter presented different ideas about the shape and the formation of the earth. This chapter leaves the world of mythology and looks at

84 · Earthbound

modern ideas about the earth. Today's scientists explain, in a very different way, some of the same things that people observed thousands of years ago. One important theory that modern scientists have developed is called *plate tectonics*. Many scientists now believe that the crust of the earth consists of different *continental plates*. These plates that form the outer layer of the earth are slowly moving. This chapter's discussion of plate tectonics will explain what happens when continental plates move. It will also explain what happens when two plates get closer to each other or even collide.

To the Student

At the end of this chapter, you will be able to

1. talk about plate tectonics;
2. understand what happens when plates move and collide; and
3. discuss topics related to earthquakes.

Vocabulary Development

Read the following list of important words from chapter 5 (you may have seen some of them in previous chapters). If you already know the word, put a check mark (✓) in the space in front of the word. When you finish the chapter, return to this list. Mark all the new words you learned. Write down additional words that you learned. (The words that are italicized here will be used in an exercise that appears later in this chapter.)

__ movement	__ existence	__ dinosaur	__ theory
__ damage	__ crust	__ core	__ mantle
__ *weight*	__ liquid	__ density	__ consistency
__ land	__ surface	__ layer	__ advance
__ break	__ *believe*	__ melt	__ *shift*
__ occur	__ meet	__ *make*	__ break
__ *drift*	__ touch	__ happen	__ *split* from
__ push up	__ move toward	__ thick	__ thin
__ solid	__ large	__ small	__ *single*
__ barely	__ quickly	__ slowly	__ *these*

_____   _____   _____   _____

_____   _____   _____   _____

_____   _____   _____   _____

_____   _____   _____   _____

The sounds you can focus on in this chapter are

[ɪ] as in g*i*ve or l*i*ve   [iː] as in sl*ee*p or pl*ea*se
[eɪ] as in r*ai*n or p*ay*

Listen especially for these sounds when you practice new words with your classmates and teacher. Look at the vocabulary list and find the italicized words that have one of the three sounds. Then write these words in the appropriate position in the chart that follows. When you are done with the chapter, try to add more words to this list.

[ɪ]	[eɪ]	[iː]

86 · Earthbound

I. Drifting Continental Plates

A. Scientists tell us that the earth didn't always look like it does today. The pictures on p. 87 show what some scientists today think about the formation of the continents. Match the pictures with the following text.

Paragraph 1.
Picture ___
Probably about 150 million years ago the single continent, Pangaea, broke into two parts, a northern continent, Laurasia, and a southern continent, Gondwanaland. Proof for the existence of these two continents was the discovery of *Lystrosaurus*. This was a dinosaur that could only live on land and was about the size of a large dog. Remains of this dinosaur were found in South Africa, India, and Antarctica.

Paragraph 2.
Picture ___
About 25 million years ago, the world looked as it does today. However, even today the continents are still drifting. Every year the Atlantic Ocean gets wider by a few inches and the Pacific Ocean gets smaller. Australia is now moving northward. In 50 million years, it will probably touch the landmass of Eurasia.

Paragraph 3.
Picture ___
Some 200 million years ago, there was probably only one continent. It is now called Pangaea. In Greek, *pan* means *all* and *gaea* means *land*. There was also only one single sea. Scientists today call it Panthalassa. This word is also of Greek origin and means *all sea*.

Paragraph 4.
Picture ___
65 million years ago, Gondwanaland was breaking up into several pieces. North America had not split from Eurasia yet, but the South Atlantic Ocean separated Africa and South America. The plates continued to move apart. Active volcanoes and earthquakes began to shape the surface of the earth.

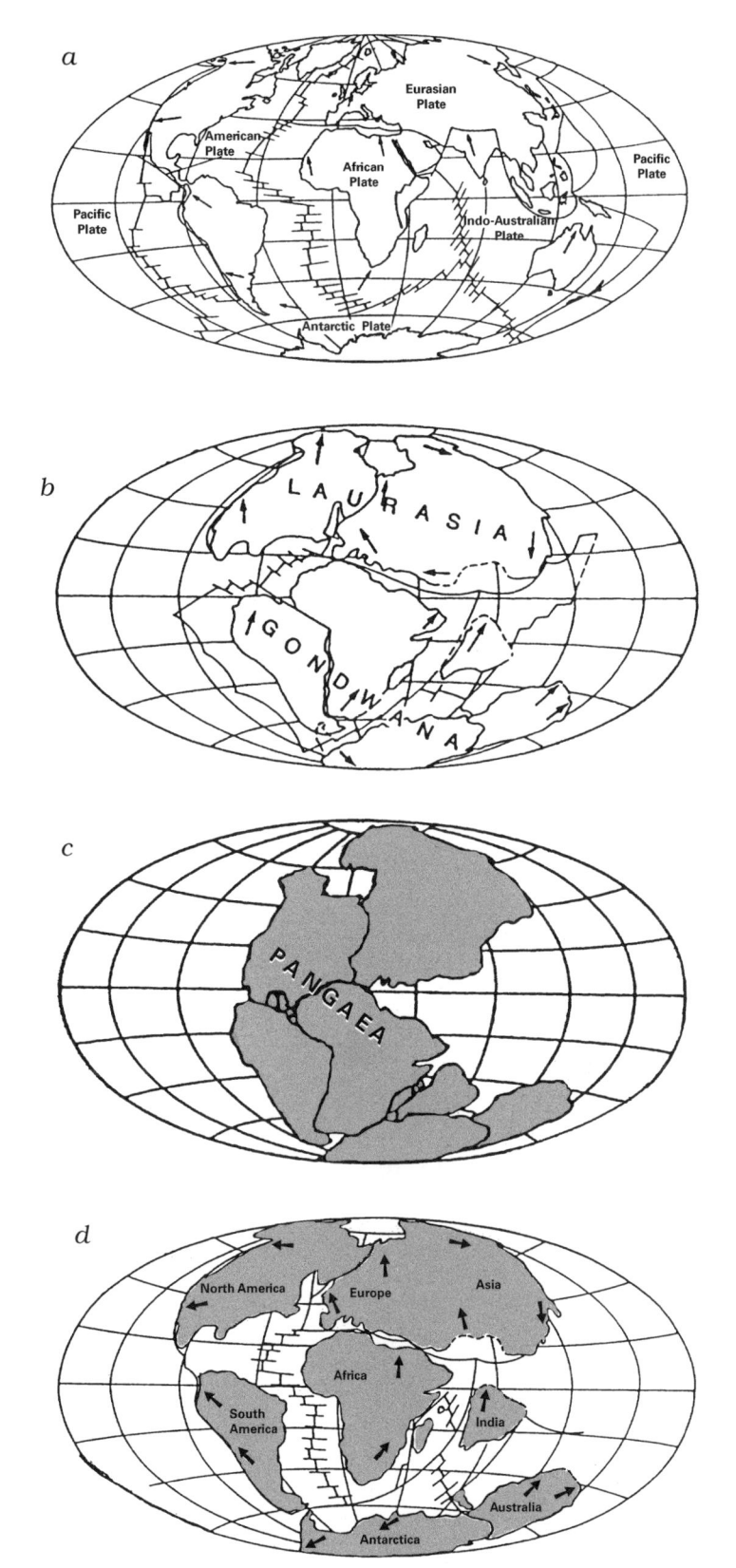

Courtesy of the American Petroleum Institute.

88 · Earthbound

B. Scan the paragraphs in Activity A to answer the following questions. Look for a *key word* and then scan the paragraph that has the information you need. Some key words are printed in italics.

1. Put the four paragraphs (1, 2, 3, 4) in the correct time order. What happened first, second and so forth?

2. How many parts did *Pangaea* break into?

3. What are the names of these *two parts*?

4. What is a *Lystrosaurus*?

5. Why can the *Lystrosaurus* show that this theory about the earth is correct?

6. What does the word *Pangaea* mean?

7. What is the name of the single sea that existed *200 million years ago*?

8. Which *ocean* gets smaller every year and which *ocean* gets wider every year?

9. What shaped the *surface* of the earth 65 million years ago?

C. Look at three important words from the next listening activity (*material, earth, and motion*). Then look at the word list and decide which of the words in the list is in any way related to the three words. Write each word from the list next to one of the three words. What other words do you associate with these nouns? Draw more lines and write related nouns and adjectives around each word.

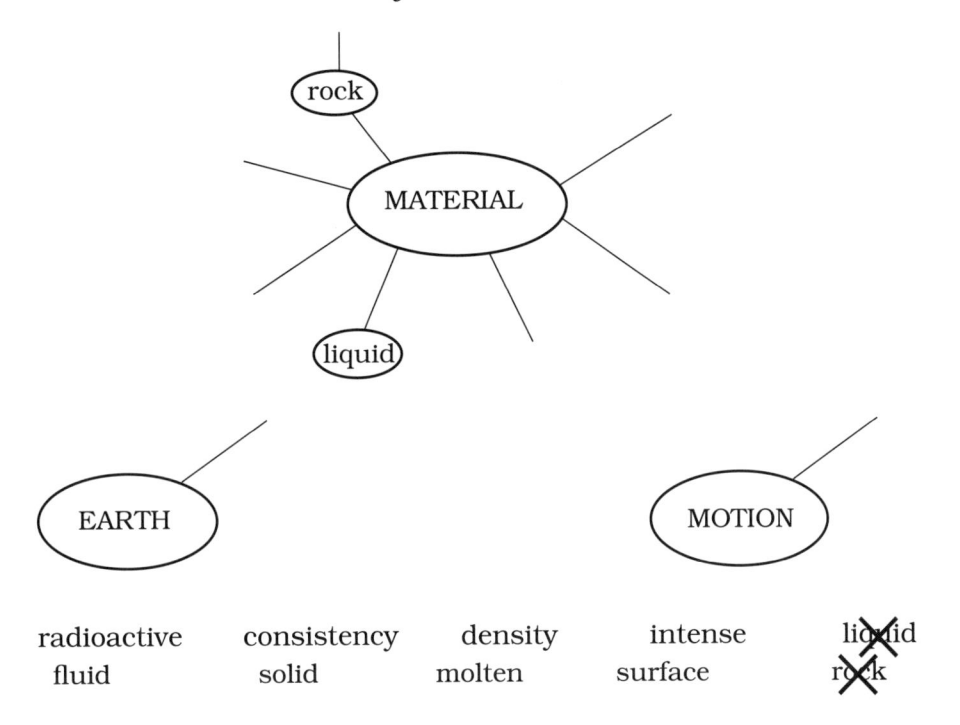

```
              rock
                \
            MATERIAL
            /   |   \
         liquid


   EARTH              MOTION
```

radioactive	consistency	density	intense	~~liquid~~
fluid	solid	molten	surface	~~rock~~

D. According to the theory of *plate tectonics*, the surface of the earth consists of continental plates. These plates move and they can also break. Let's find out why that happens.

1. Look at the picture and listen to the beginning of a lecture. What is the lecture about?

2. Listen to the complete lecture and write down the names of the three zones shown in the picture.

90 · **Earthbound**

3. Label the figure.

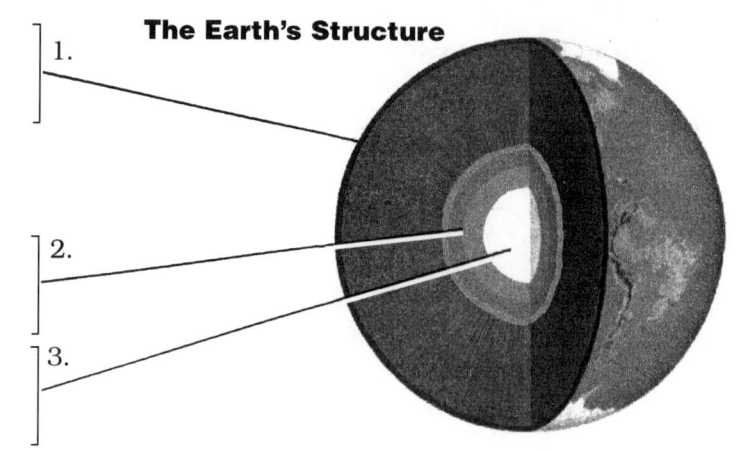

The Earth's Structure

1. _____
2. _____
3. _____

From H. H. Gross, *World Geography* (Englewood Cliffs, NJ: Prentice Hall, 1980).

E. Now listen to the lecture on plate tectonics again and fill in the chart.

	Name	Thickness	*Liquid or Solid Material*
1. _____ a. b. oceanic crust	a. b.	a. solid b.
2. _____	1,740 miles	
3. _____ a. b.	a. b.	a. b.

F. With the information you have in the chart for Activity E, fill in the blanks with the correct forms of the words.

thin   hot   thick   hard

1. The outer layer of the earth is _____ than all other zones.

2. The center of the earth is _____ than the mantle.

3. The continental crust is _____ than the oceanic crust.

4. The mantle is _____ than the crust.

5. The inner core is _____ than the outer core.

G. We learned why the continental plates are moving. Let's look at possible results of the movement. Complete each paragraph with the appropriate ending (a, b, or c). Be ready to explain why you chose the ending.
   When you are done, try to find these places on the map.

| a. This ocean between South America and Africa is now called the South Atlantic Ocean. | b. Today the Indian plate still continues its slow advance beneath Asia. It pushes the Himalayas up. These peaks rise about 2 inches higher each year. | c. It marks a break in the continent where the African plate is splitting apart. Along this break an ocean arm like the Red Sea may develop. |

1. The Great Rift Valley of eastern Africa was formed a long time ago. This valley stretches some 2,500 miles from the Red Sea to Mozambique. _____

92 · Earthbound

2. About 135 million years ago, South America and Africa started to separate along a break in the earth's crust. This rift turned into a big ocean. _____

   _____

   _____

3. 65 million years ago, India was still on its journey toward Asia. Many hundred years later the Indian plate and the Asian plate collided, or touched each other. _____

   _____

   _____

H. Which words in Activity G helped you find the correct ending for each paragraph?

_____

_____

Cohesive Devices

Words that help readers understand the structure of a text are called *cohesive devices*. Pronouns that function as cohesive devices have been discussed in chapter 4. Other cohesive devices are, for example, synonyms or generalizing words.

In the following examples the cohesive device is italicized and an arrow is drawn to its referent:

Pronoun	Geographers study the earth. *They* also study the people who live on *it*.
Synonym	Hawaii is very different from other states in the United States. *The Aloha State* is a chain of volcanic islands.
General Word	The earth is very special. *This planet* is the only one in the solar system that can support life.

I. Go back to Activity G and find all the cohesive devices in the completed paragraphs. Then draw an arrow from each cohesive device to its referent (see examples in language box).

II. Earthquakes

A. Look at the world map and the title of the reading passage in Activity B. What do you think the passage will be about?

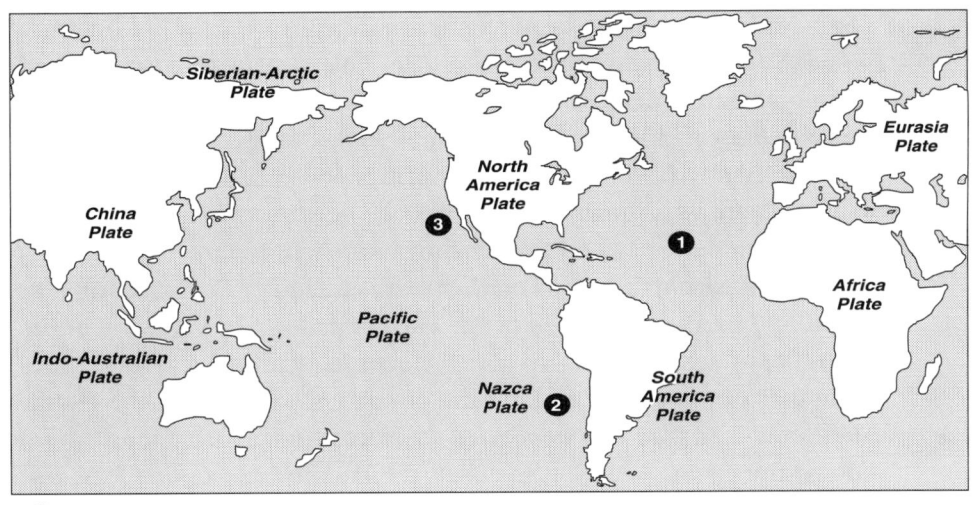

❶ Earthquakes happen where plates move apart (North America–Africa plates).
❷ Earthquakes happen where plates collide (Nazca–South America plates).
❸ Earthquakes happen where plates move past each other (North America–Pacific plates).

B. The following expressions are found in the reading passage "Fractures in the Solid Rock." What do you think these expressions mean? Discuss your ideas and then read the passage to find out.

a. the ring of fire
b. Richter scale

FRACTURES IN THE SOLID ROCK

The theory of plate tectonics explains why the surface of the earth changes constantly. Due to radioactive rocks, the heat inside the earth can rise above 1,700°F (900°C). This heat turns the rock in the top part of the mantle into a thick liquid. The Earth's crust floats on this hot liquid just like a piece of wood floats on water.

The heat produced in the mantle not only turns the rocks into a thick liquid, but it also makes this liquid move. So, the continental crust is floating on molten rock that is constantly moving. As a result of the movement in the mantle, the crustal plates can break. Imagine the earth as a huge egg with a cracked shell.

The fractures in the solid rock of the earth's crust are called faults. A spectacular example of a fault is the San Andreas fault in California. The land east of the San Andreas fault is slowly but steadily moving south. Sometimes it moves so much that the underlying rock breaks and an earthquake occurs. On April 18, 1906, the ground shifted as much as 15 1/2 feet along 200 miles of the San Andreas fault. This movement caused an earthquake with a magnitude of 6.9 on the Richter scale. This earthquake demolished much of San Francisco. It was one of the biggest earth shifts ever recorded for a single quake. On October 17, 1989, the area was hit by another earthquake. This time it reached 7.1 on the Richter scale. There was, however, less damage because modern constructions were better suited to withstand an earthquake.

Nearly all earthquakes on Earth are caused by the fracturing, or breaking, of the solid rock of the earth's crust. The majority of the significant earthquakes on Earth begin in two long narrow zones. The main zone is a belt along the countries that border the Pacific Ocean. It runs up the west coast of North and South America and down the coast of Asia. It is called the Pacific "ring of fire" because most of the world's volcanoes are along its path. The Pacific belt is also the site of about 80 percent of all earthquakes on Earth. The second major zone runs from west to east across Europe and Asia to join the Pacific belt. This zone includes Spain, northern Africa, Italy, Greece, Turkey, India, and Burma. This zone is responsible for an additional 15 percent of the earthquakes on Earth. The remaining quakes occur at scattered locations around the globe.

C. Draw the ring of fire on the world map on page 93.

D. A "Word Quake" mixed up the letters of some words that are important for this chapter. Most of them were used in the reading passage "Fractures in the Solid Rock." Try to form words with the letters given and write them on the blank lines above the definitions.

1. qartuakehe _____
   (a sudden shaking of the earth's surface)

2. mtnigudea _____
   (greatness of size or importance)

3. oviletn _____
   (acting with great damaging force)

4. acolpsel _____
   (the act of falling down or inward)

5. kosem _____
   (something that is produced during a fire)

6. ademag _____
   (harm or loss)

7. ernepicet _____
   (the point on the earth's surface directly above the quake's origin)

8. condestruti _____
   (the act of destroying something)

9. cocru _____
   (to happen or take place)

10. tble _____
    (a zone that has some special quality)

11. orredc _____
    (to write down or take note of something)

12. modelish _____
    (to destroy completely)

13. tufracer _____
    (the act or result of breaking something)

96 · Earthbound

14. sttedcaer _____
   (an adjective for small and far apart)

15. tahp _____
   (a line along which something moves)

E. Are the following statements about the reading passage "Fractures in the Solid Rock" true or false? For each statement write true (T) or false (F) in the answer blank.

1. The heat produced in the mantle makes the continental plates move. __
2. The earth looks like a giant egg with a cracked shell. __
3. The crustal plates break because they get so hot. __
4. The land mass east of the San Andreas fault is slowly moving north. __
5. In 1906 the United States experienced one of the biggest earth shifts ever recorded for a single quake. __
6. All earthquakes are caused by fracturing of the solid rock of the crust. __
7. The principal earthquake zone is near the Atlantic Ocean. __
8. The Pacific "ring of fire" can be seen as a black ring on the ground. __

F. Look at these phrases that tell facts from the reading passage and say which of the two conditions has to exist first to make the other condition possible—or which of the two situations is the *reason*.

	Condition A	*Condition B*
1.	radioactive rocks produce heat _1_	the top part of the mantle melts _2_
2.	the mantle consists of hot liquid rock __	the crust floats __
3.	deep valleys occur __	crustal plates pull away from each other __
4.	deep oceans arise __	the edge of one plate plunges under another __

5. one plate is dragged past another ___   large faults occur ___
6. the rock fractures or breaks ___   earthquakes occur ___
7. there are volcanoes along its path ___   the zone is called the ring of fire ___
8. the ground shifts ___   earthquakes occur ___

G. Activity F showed the difference between a *reason/cause* and an *effect*. The English language uses certain words to express cause/effect relationships in one sentence.
Look at the following sentence formed from example 1 in Activity F and answer the questions.

The top part of the mantle melts because radioactive rocks produce heat.

1. Which part of the sentence shows the cause?

2. Which part shows the effect?

3. How are the two parts of the sentence connected?

98 · Earthbound

Cause and Effect in a Complex Sentence

Complex sentences are sentences that have a *main,* or *independent, clause* and at least one *dependent clause.*

An *independent clause* has a subject + a verb and can stand alone. It is a complete sentence.

1. The rocks melt.
2. The temperature is very high.   simple sentences

A *dependent clause* also has a subject + a verb, but alone it is not complete. It depends on the main clause.

. . . because the temperature is very high . . .

The rocks melt because the temperature is very high. complex sentence
    effect   cause
(independent   (dependent clause)
  clause)

Note

The word *because* is one way to begin a dependent clause. This word always introduces the cause and not the effect.

Since cause and effect form one sentence, there is no punctuation mark between them!

You can say, however:

Because the temperature is very high, the rocks melt.
               cause   effect

(If you begin a sentence with the cause, you need to add a comma after the cause.)

H. Look at the sentence fragments in Activity F. Combine each pair into a single sentence using the word *because.*

Example:

radioactive rocks produce heat <u>1</u> the top part of the mantle melts <u>2</u>

The top part of the mantle melts because radioactive rocks produce heat.

I. How are earthquakes measured? Look at the chart on page 100 and put the four descriptions (a, b, c, d) that were left out from the Mercali scale in their appropriate place in the chart. Use the italicized adjectives to help you.

   a. *moderate:* windows rattle
   b. *disastrous:* widespread damage, landslides, steel bends
   c. *strong:* poorly constructed buildings destroyed, others damaged (e.g., walls crack)
   d. *feeble:* felt by people resting

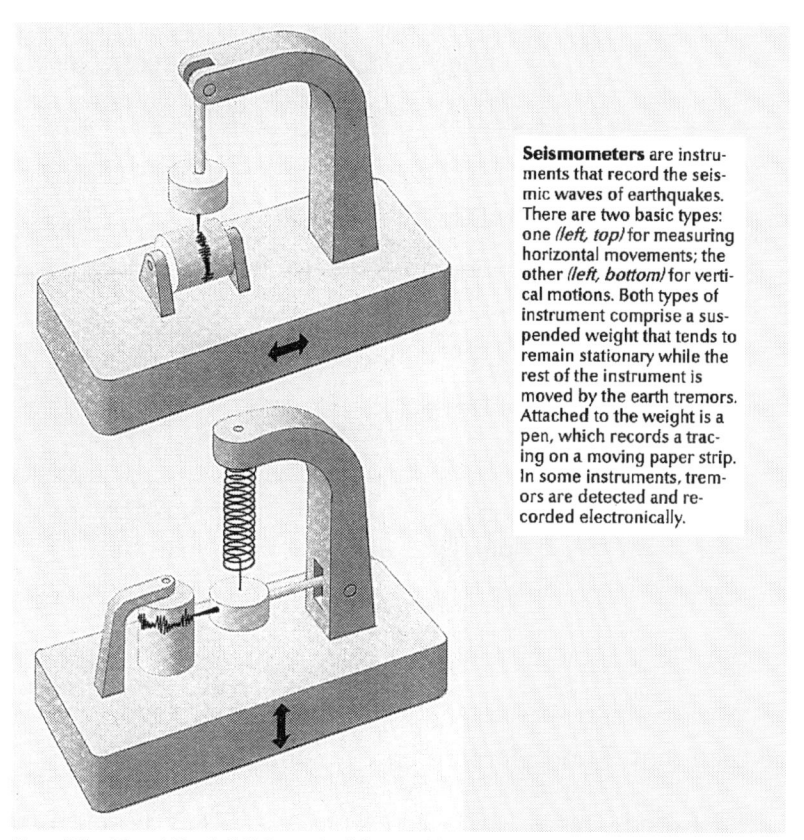

Seismometers are instruments that record the seismic waves of earthquakes. There are two basic types: one *(left, top)* for measuring horizontal movements; the other *(left, bottom)* for vertical motions. Both types of instrument comprise a suspended weight that tends to remain stationary while the rest of the instrument is moved by the earth tremors. Attached to the weight is a pen, which records a tracing on a moving paper strip. In some instruments, tremors are detected and recorded electronically.

From "The Planet Earth," Volume 4 of the *World Book Encyclopedia of Science.* © 1989 Verlagsruppe Bertelsmann International. By permission of World Book, Inc.

Richter Scale (Expresses *magnitude* of the earthquake. It is measured at the center of the earthquake, the epicenter. Each increment of a whole number signifies a 10-fold increase in magnitude.)	Mercali Scale (Expresses the *intensity* of an earthquake, or the damage levels in terms of the consequences that are felt or seen in populated areas. This scale describes probable effects that earthquakes, occurring near the earth's surface, can have on humans.)
<3	not felt or barely detectable even near the epicenter; detectable only by instruments
3–3.4	
3.5–4	slight: like heavy trucks passing
4.1–4.4	
4.5–4.8	rather strong: wakes sleeping people, may cause slight damage (e.g., windows break)
4.9–5.4	
5.5–6	very strong: people fall over, buildings crack
6.1–6.5	moderately destructive: chimneys fall, buildings move
6.6–7	ruinous: heavy damage to buildings, ground cracks
7.1–7.3	
7.4–8.1	very disastrous: nearly total damage with pipelines and railroads breaking.
>8.1	catastrophic: total destruction

Adapted from *Visual Factfinder: Planet Earth* by Neil Curtis and Michael Allaby, copyright © Grisewood & Dempsey Ltd. 1993. Reprinted with permission of Larousse Kingfisher Chambers Inc., New York.

J. Use the Richter and Mercali scales to answer the questions.

1. Earthquakes can be measured in two ways. Which scale uses numbers to express the magnitude of an earthquake?

2. The intensity of earthquakes can be expressed by describing probable effects. What is the name of this type of scale?

3. Can you feel an earthquake of 1.5 on the Richter scale?

4. What happens during an earthquake that reaches 5.0 on the Richter scale?

5. Which word expresses more damage: *ruinous* or *catastrophic*?

6. Complete the sentence with the correct number.
A magnitude 5 earthquake produces an effect that is ___ times higher than a magnitude 4 earthquake.

7. What does the actual impact of an earthquake depend on (besides its severity)? Do you think that today's earthquakes are more destructive than they were hundreds of years ago? Why or why not?

8. Do you think that the following statement is true? Explain why.
Every earthquake has just one Richter magnitude, but it has many intensities.

III. When an Earthquake Hits!

A. Think about the following questions. Then tell your classmates about your ideas.

1. Have you ever experienced an earthquake? What was it like?

2. What would you do if someone told you that by the end of this year there would be an earthquake in your area?

B. Read the following newspaper article.

Experts Say Major Earthquake to Hit Eastern U.S.

1 Most Americans think that major earthquakes take place in the
2 Western states. But scientists say the U.S. east of the Rocky Moun-
3 tains will someday have a big earthquake.
4 The big danger comes from the New Madrid fault zone, located
5 in portions of Missouri, Arkansas, and Tennessee.
6 According to the director of the Tennessee Earthquake Informa-
7 tion Center, Arch Johnson, "Possibly within our lifetime, possibly
8 many generations from now, a destructive earthquake will occur in
9 the Eastern United States."
10 The New Madrid seismic zone is its most likely site. This zone
11 first drew attention in the winter of 1811–1812 when three giant
12 earthquakes there made bells ring as far away as Boston.
13 The quakes in 1811–1812 measured 8.4 on the Richter scale.
14 Officials say that any earthquake in that part of the country today
15 measuring 8.0 or more would cause damage of $50 billion. Millions
16 of people would be killed or injured.
17 Experts say that in the event of an earthquake, you should stay
18 away from windows, mirrors, and chimneys because they can fall
19 down and hit you. It is usually best not to run outside. Their advice
20 is to stay indoors and to take cover under a desk or bed or to stand
21 beneath the frame of a doorway. People who live in an earthquake
22 area may want to keep a flashlight and sturdy shoes by their beds,
23 so they can get to safety even when an earthquake hits at night.
24 Safety officials also say it's not wise to use elevators during
25 earthquakes since the power may fail. Do not rush to exits in public
26 buildings since there may be a stampede.
27 People outdoors in an earthquake are advised to stay away from
28 tall buildings and utility poles. Drivers of cars or trucks should stop
29 as soon as possible. An open space is best.

Adapted from H.F. Decker, *Newspaper Workshop* (New York: Globe Book Company, 1985).

C. Find a word or phrase that you could use instead of each of the following words or phrases from the article "Experts Say Major Earthquake to Hit Eastern U.S."

1. major (line 1) _____

2. portions (line 5) _____

3. possibly (line 7) _____

4. occur (line 8) _____

5. site (line 10) _____

6. giant (line 11) _____

7. stay away from (lines 17–18) _____

8. take cover under (line 20) _____

9. it's not wise (line 24) _____

10. Do not rush (line 25) _____

11. are advised to (line 27) _____

12. tall (line 28) _____

D. Answer the following questions about the passage.

1. According to the article, what do most Americans think about earthquakes?

2. Where is the New Madrid fault zone located?

3. What does Arch Johnson believe?

4. What was the magnitude of the earthquake that occurred in 1811 in the New Madrid fault zone?

5. How much damage would a similar earthquake cause today?

6. Do the safety officials believe that it is a good idea to leave the house during an earthquake?

E. Look at the reading passage in Activity B and make a list of things people should or should not do during an earthquake. When you are done, explain to a partner why he or she should or should not do certain things during an earthquake. Can you think of more advice to give?

The Modals Should / Ought to and Can

1. The modal auxiliaries *should* and *ought to* are used in English to give advice. They are placed before the base form of the verb. To express a negative idea, use *should not*.
   Note: Ought to is normally not used in negative statements or questions.

   Example:

   Drivers of cars or trucks *should stop* as soon as possible during an earthquake.
   Drivers of cars or trucks *ought to stop* immediately during an earthquake.
   Should drivers continue their trip? No, they *shouldn't* continue it.

2. The modal *can* has two different meanings.
   a. *Can* expresses *ability in the present*. The negative form is *can't (cannot)* and the past tense form is *couldn't (could not)*.

   Example:

   You *can* feel an earthquake. You *can't* drive during an earthquake. I *couldn't* sleep during the earthquake.

   b. *Can* and *could* also express *possibility in the future*.

   Example:

   Scientists predict that we *can* expect an earthquake east of the Rocky Mountains.
   Someday there *could* be an earthquake east of the Rocky Mountains.

F. You are going to read a newspaper article about an earthquake in China. Before you start reading, list the type of information you want to find in the article. Then read the article.

Earthbound

> CHINA SHAKEN BY SECOND EARTHQUAKE IN TWO WEEKS!
>
> Hong Kong—An earthquake with a magnitude of 6.2 struck Tuesday, January 10, off the coast of southern China. This is the second quake to hit the area in less than two weeks. A dispatch by China's official Xinua News Agency mentioned no casualties. It said residents described the shaking as more violent than a quake in the same area on December 31. That quake, also with a magnitude of 6.2, injured 50 people. According to the Royal Hong Kong Observatory, Tuesday's quake in the Gulf of Tonkin was recorded at 6:11 P.M. and was centered 74 miles west-northwest of the coastal city of Haikou on Hainan Island. A quake with a magnitude of 6 can cause heavy damage in populated areas.

(From the Associated Press in the *State News*, Wednesday, January 11, 1995)

G. Fill in the chart with the information given in the newspaper article "China Shaken by Second Earthquake in Two Weeks!"

Location	Date/Time	Magnitude	Effects

H. This reporter's notes about an earthquake in Japan were mixed up and partly lost. Try to reconstruct them and write a newspaper article about the earthquake. Make sure you group and organize the pieces of information before you start writing.

powerful predawn earthquake   magnitude of 7.2   smoke

densely populated   death toll rose to 4,614   5:46 a.m.   major

port of 1.4 million people

25,226 people injured   Tuesday, January 10   trains derailed

The Earth in Motion · 107

    power knocked out   elevated expressway collapsed

    most violent in two decades   fires   underground pipes burst

    water   western Japan

        city of Kobe   280 miles west of Tokyo

I. Twenty words from the chapter are hidden in the rectangle. Look from left to right and top to bottom. When you find a word, draw a circle around it. Make a list of all the words you find. Put them into groups according to the part of speech they belong to (noun, verb, or adjective).

```
R L I Q U I D P B I N K E L M T I L
C D E G S Y X W O P E B Z A A D T C
O Q U S U R F A C E C R U S T I X O
R A P P R O P R I A T E O Y E S P N
E Q E L A S L O M B X A M E R C V T
K S A I G U A I R C H K X M I O L I
C H K T X S T R E T C H O A A V X N
D A V J R O E F P U S H I N L E N U
A P C O L L I D E A C E N T E R O E
J E P E X I S T E N C E M L X Y L U
Z E F G I D L A Q K I W E E P U S R
```

Nouns:

Verbs:

Adjectives:

Chapter 6

The Land

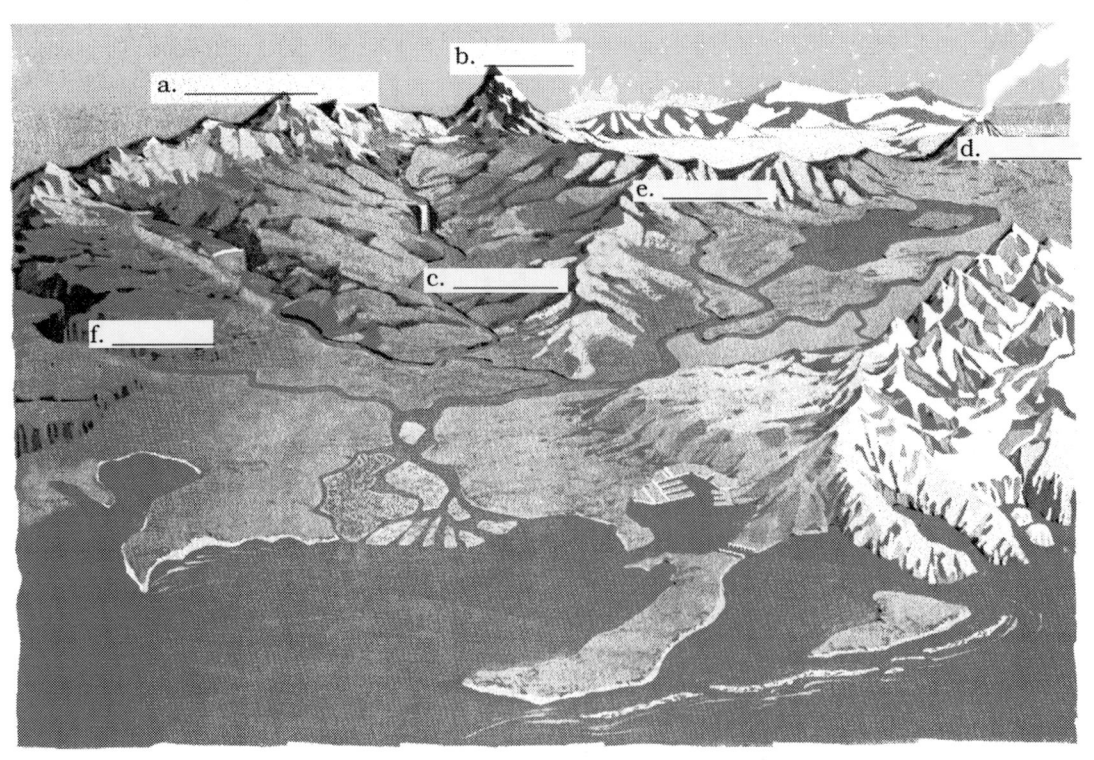

a. _____
b. _____
c. _____
d. _____
e. _____
f. _____

From H.H. Gross, *World Geography* (Englewood Cliffs, NJ: Prentice Hall, 1980).

Look at the picture and write the name for each land formation on the blank lines provided. Use the following definition of the word to find the correct object in the picture.

108

canyon: a very deep and narrow valley

divide: a mountain range that separates river systems

mountain range: a chain of mountains

peak: the top of a high mountain, or mountain in general

valley: lower area between mountain ranges

volcano: a hole in the surface of the earth through which rock and ash can come up

A Look Behind/A Look Ahead

The previous three chapters focused on the study of the earth from an ancient and from a modern perspective. Most importantly, the discussion of plate tectonics showed how various forces shaped the earth. Now that we have learned about the forces within the earth, the next three chapters will investigate in more detail the things that humans can see and experience on the surface of the earth. The focus will be on the physical and human geography of Planet Earth, and, of course, a lot of time will be spent on *explaining* all the things that happen on Earth. We begin in chapter 6 with natural landforms. This chapter looks at mountains and volcanoes and shows how they are created and how they affect life on Earth.

To the Student

At the end of this chapter, you will be able to

1. describe how mountains are formed;
2. understand the effects of volcanoes; and
3. discuss how important mountains are to humans.

Vocabulary Development

Read the following list of important words from chapter 6 (you may have seen some of them in previous chapters). If you already know the word, put a check mark (✓) in the space in front of the word. When you finish the chapter, return to this list. Mark all the new words you learned. Write down additional words that you learned.

110 · Earthbound

___ mountain range ___ explosion ___ force ___ lava
___ divide ___ magma ___ erosion ___ fault
___ location ___ pebbles ___ growth ___ soil
___ rocks ___ edge ___ process ___ slope
___ valley ___ decay ___ crack ___ flood
___ erupt ___ blow ___ grow ___ erode
___ fold ___ remove ___ wear down ___ carve
___ expand ___ contract ___ crumble ___ tumble
___ gradual ___ artificial ___ steep ___ quickly

_____ _____ _____ _____

_____ _____ _____ _____

_____ _____ _____ _____

In this section you will review some of the vocabulary you have learned so far and learn some important words for this chapter. Read the sentences and circle the word that completes each sentence correctly. If you don't know a word, look it up in your dictionary.

1. Metal can _____.
   fail   contract   strong   believe

2. Wood can _____.
   cut   drink   wear down   heavy

3. Rocks can _____.
   erode   represent   burn   study

4. Ice can _____.
   dream   crack   different   freeze

5. Bread can _____.
   damage   happen   develop   crumble

6. Heated iron can _____.
   bare   expand   tiny   split from

7. Leaves can _____.
    decay   advance   happen   push up

8. Wind can be _____.
    steady   long   happy   afraid

9. A person can _____ a rock.
    lift up   kill   consist of

10. In the mountains, water can _____ from a rock and form a waterfall.
    swim   plunge down   survive

11. The Suez Canal connects the Mediterranean and the Red Sea. It is called a(n) _____ waterway because it was made by people and not by nature.
    artificial   tiny   included

12. Water can _____ holes into stone.
    carve   live   revolve

13. The word _____ is another term for border.
    crust   edge   surface

14. When you make the ground wet, _____ does not rise.
    dust   rain   work

15. The _____ within the earth is responsible for earthquakes.
    noise   damage   pressure

112 · **Earthbound**

I. Mountains

A. Look at the world map and the description of the mountain ranges in the world. Write down the number of the mountain range next to its description.

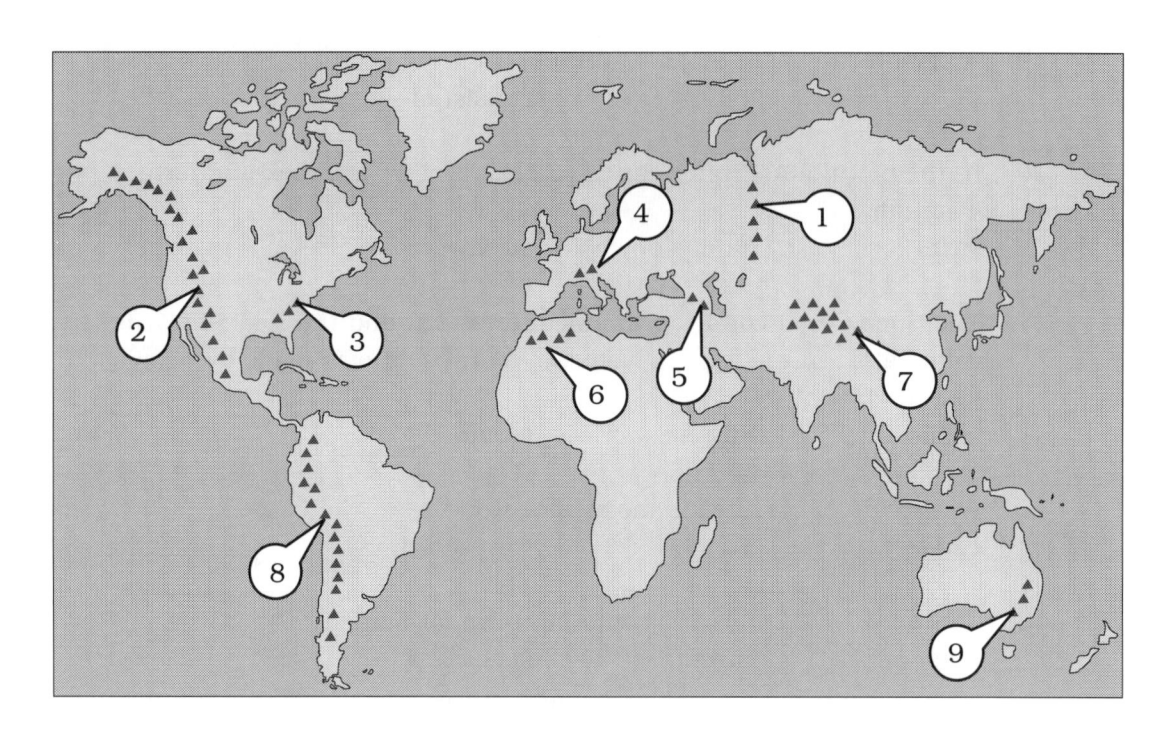

___ Alps
(a mountain range in Europe)
___ Andes
(mountains in the southern part of the American continent)
___ Appalachian Mountains
(mountains north of the Andes)

___ Atlas
(a mountain range in the northwestern part of the African continent)
___ Caucasus
(mountains to the northeast of the Atlas mountains)
___ Great Dividing Range
(the only mountain range in Australia)

___ Himalayas
(a very big mountain range in Asia)
___ Rocky Mountains
(a mountain range in the western part of the North-American continent)
___ Urals
(a mountain range in Eastern Europe)

B. Listen to the speaker talk about mountains in different countries and write the correct numbers on the blank lines.

Name (Country)	Height (in feet)	Name (Country)	Height (in feet)
Kilimanjaro (Tanzania)	_____	Mount Everest (border of Nepal and Tibet)	_____
Kosciusko (Australia)	7,316	Elbrus (Caucasus)	18,481
Guallatiri (Chile)	19,882	Mt. Wilhelm (New Guinea)	_____
Mont Blanc (Switzerland)	_____	Cotopaxi (Ecuador)	19,642
Fujiyama (Japan)	_____	Mauna Kea (Hawaii) (measured from the ocean floor)	_____
Nanga Parbat (India)	26,660	Mount McKinley or Denali (Alaska)	20,320
		Mount Aconcagua (Argentina)	22,834

C. Read the passage "Earth's Mountains" and fill in the words you expect to find in the blank spaces.

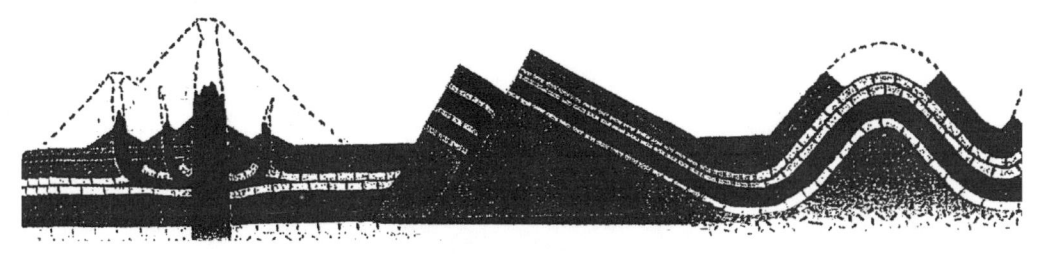

    volcano   block mountain   folded mountain

Earth's Mountains

The shape of a mountain depends on three things: how it was formed, its age, and erosion. Mountains are generally made of material from the earth's _____. This material is lifted and lowered by the motion within the earth. Pressures inside the earth can build _____ in three different _____.

The first way is folding. Heat, radioactivity, shifting weight, or other yet unknown forces within the earth's _____ _____ put pressure on some areas of the earth's crust. As a result, the rock may arch or fold. The best _____ _____ of folded mountains in the United States today _____ _____ the Appalachians, near the Atlantic coast.

The _____ way mountains are built is by faulting. Sometimes, the pressure in the earth is so high that the rock can't bend anymore and simply breaks. This _____ _____ is along the crust's weakest place. "Fault" is the word used to speak of a line of weakness in the crust. When pressure occurs at a fault, it may _____ the rock on one side of the fault upward as one piece, or block. The Sierra Nevadas are a _____ example of block mountains made by faulting.

The third _____ of mountains are those caused by volcanoes. Usually it takes many volcanic _____ _____ to make a mountain, but sometimes the mountain is built quickly. In 1943 a new volcano exploded in a Mexican field, and within a few years this mountain grew to 1,500 feet. That is about one-third the height of the _____ Italian volcano, Vesuvius, which has been building slowly over hundreds of years. Mount Parícutin, the Mexican volcano, has now stopped growing. Many volcanoes _____ beautifully shaped mountains with steep slopes. Fujiyama in Japan and Mauna Loa in Hawaii, for example, are almost perfect cones.

D. Practice the new words that were used in Activity C. Circle the most correct answer.

1. It is easy to imagine that one can fold paper but it is not easy to imagine _____ rocks.

    a. folding
    b. hard
    c. gray

2. If one side of a mountain is lifted up higher than the other, the mountain looks like it is _____.

    a. soft
    b. dusty
    c. tilted

3. The _____ of a mountain that is facing south gets more sunlight than the one that is facing north.

    a. slope
    b. temperature
    c. force

4. Most of the famous volcanoes in the world have the shape of a(n) _____.

    a. arm
    b. fist
    c. cone

5. The word _____ means the same as the phrase *wear away*.

    a. lift
    b. lower
    c. erode

E. The following paragraphs are the continuation of the reading passage "Earth's Mountains." Read the sentences and the paragraphs. Find out what each paragraph is about and write the best topic sentence on the blank line.

Paragraph 1

a. Some mountains are smaller than others because the eroding goes on faster.
b. Outward forces erode the mountains, or wear them away.
c. What keeps the mountains from growing and growing?

_____

_____. At the same time that mountains begin to grow because of crustal movement, erosion wears them away. For example, the Appalachian Mountains, now about 2,000 to 6,000 feet above sea level, have been uplifted and worn down at least three times. The building up and the eroding go on at the same time. Most mountains grow so slowly that the eroding sometimes goes on faster than the mountain develops. The mountains are worn down steadily by the forces of erosion: wind, rain, moving water, and ice, as well as temperature and chemical change.

Paragraph 2

a. In mountain areas, streams and rivers cut U-shaped valleys into the stone.
b. The solid rock of mountains is cut off by steep waterfalls.
c. All through the mountain areas, water changes the shape of the rocks.

_____

_____. Most water erosion on mountains is caused by streams and rivers that plunge down the steep sides. The rivers lift up rocks and push them along. These rocks rub and scrape against other rocks. As a result, the rivers cut V-shaped valleys into the mountains. Sometimes tumbling water can make deep potholes in solid rock. In other areas, waterfalls sometimes cut the edges off cliffs.

Paragraph 3

a. In cold areas, slowly moving rivers of ice, called glaciers, also carve away at mountains.
b. This kind of glacier shapes the mountains by pushing small pebbles, soil, and big rocks forward.

c. Some materials become fixed in the ice of the glacier and cut U-shaped valleys into the rock.

_____. They are formed when heavy snows accumulate on the top of the mountains and are pressed into ice. Like a giant arm with a big fist at its end, a glacier pushes rocks, pebbles, soil, and boulders as it goes. These materials become fixed in the ice of the glacier at its sides, middle, and forward end. They act as mighty carving agents and cut a U-shaped valley down the mountain. Glaciers move at a rate of a few inches to a few feet a day in summer. Since they carry with them rock dust, they also shape the slope of a mountain.

F. Following are paragraphs 4 and 5 of the reading passage "Earth's Mountains." These paragraphs are also about the forces that shape mountains. Find out what force each paragraph is about. Then write a possible topic sentence on the blank line.

Paragraph 4

  Topic: _____

_____. Rocks expand daily in the heat of the sun and then contract again during the cold nights. These constant temperature changes begin to crack the rock. Water gets into the tiny cracks, freezes at night, expands, and opens the cracks wider. As a result, the rocks may break into pieces, even crumble into soil. The wind then blows some of that soil away.

Paragraph 5

  Topic: _____

_____. People cut lanes for electric lines. They build high dams. They build roads and trails. All these actions remove the rocks, soil, and trees from the earth's surface and create artificial channels for running water, for frost and ice, and for quickly growing plants. Chemicals from air and water and decaying plants also erode the rocks.

G. Practice the new words that were used in Activities E and F. Circle the best answer.

1. Sand is made when rocks or shells scrape and _____ against each other.

    a. carry
    b. rub
    c. fix

2. Waterfalls occur when water falls, or _____ down, from a rock or cliff.

    a. expands
    b. tumbles
    c. blows

3. Small round stones in rivers or in the sea are called _____.

    a. soil
    b. boulders
    c. pebbles

4. During the Ice Age, glaciers _____ valleys in different parts of the world.

    a. carved
    b. melted
    c. happened

5. During winter snow _____ on top of the mountain. In the spring all this snow melts and often causes floods in the valleys.

    a. accumulates
    b. rises
    c. happens

6. With warm hands you can _____ snow into a ball and turn it into ice.

    a. move
    b. affect
    c. press

7. Many kinds of metals become greater in size, or _____, when they get warm.

   a. heavier
   b. expand
   c. shift

8. Frost can break rocks into very small pieces. Then the rock can _____ into soil.

   a. melt
   b. crumble
   c. build

9. When plants die and rot, we usually say that they are _____

   a. chemical
   b. eroded
   c. decayed

10. The word _____ is the opposite of expand.

    a. contract
    b. force
    c. fixed

H. Answer the questions about the complete passage "Earth's Mountains" (Activities C, D, and E).

1. What does the shape of a mountain depend on?

2. Name two ways in which mountains are formed.

3. Name three forces of erosion.

4. How is a pothole made?

5. When you look at a valley, how do you know it was shaped by a glacier and not by a river?

I. Are the following statements about the complete passage "Earth's Mountains" (Activities C, D, and E) true or false? To see how much you have learned, try to decide without looking back at the text. For each statement write true (T) or false (F) in the answer blank.

1. The two processes of building and eroding go on at the same time. ___

2. Temperature and chemical changes are the most important factors in the erosion process. ___

3. Rivers cut U-shaped valleys into the mountains. ___

4. Water that runs down the slopes of a mountain gives it its shape. ___

5. A glacier forces pebbles to build mountains. ___

6. Glaciers never move more than a few inches every day. ___

7. Rocks expand in hot temperatures. ___

8. Heavy winds in the mountains blow all rocks away. ___

9. Many things that humans do affect the erosion of a mountain. ___

II. Volcanoes

A. The italicized words in the sentences will be used in the next activity. Try to guess their meanings from the sentences given. Write your explanation for the word on the line underneath.

1. The *molten* rock that comes out of a volcano is called lava.

   _____

2. Many volcanoes are *invisible* because they are under water in the oceans.

   _____

3. A volcano is an opening in the earth's surface through which lava and other materials *erupt*.

   _____

4. Some volcanoes may lie *dormant* for many centuries between eruptions.

   _____

5. When Mount St. Helens exploded, thick clouds of hot *ash* rose to the sky.

   _____

B. You will now hear a dictation about volcanoes. Write down the sentences on a separate piece of paper as you hear them.

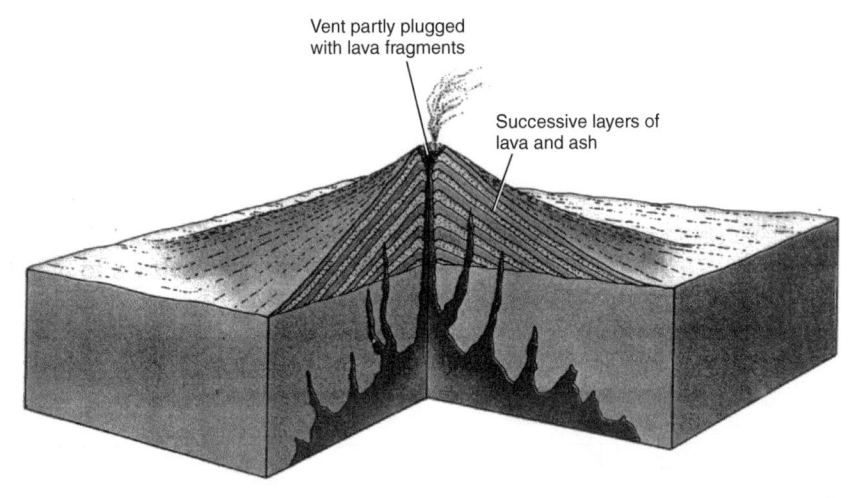

Vent partly plugged with lava fragments

Successive layers of lava and ash

From Arthur Getis, Judith Getis, and Jerome Fellman, *Introduction to Geography,* 3d ed. Copyright © 1991 Times Mirror Higher Education Group, Inc., Dubuque, Iowa. All Rights Reserved. Reprinted by permission.

C. Based on the information from the dictation in Activity B and your own experience answer the questions.

1. Does the text say how many volcanoes there are on Earth?

2. Where do volcanoes usually occur?

3. What do you call a volcano that is not active?

4. What happens when a volcano erupts?

5. What is the difference between magma and lava?

D. Take a look at the text you wrote for the dictation in Activity B. Were the prepositions difficult to hear during the dictation? Circle all the prepositions you can find. Group them according to any category you can come up with.

Prepositions of Time and Space
You studied some spatial prepositions in chapter 2. Here are examples of other important prepositions.

1. *Time*

at →	times of the day, including midnight, noon, sunrise, and sunset
on →	dates and days of the week
in →	months, year, seasons, and periods of the day like the *morning* or *evening*
for →	shows duration

(The explosion happened *at* 1:00 P.M. *on* Dec. 8 *in* 1994. I was in the hospital *for* three weeks.)

2. *Space and Direction*

in →	*in* the house, *in* the streets, *in* the state, *in* English
inside →	*inside* the building (when the interior of a structure is thought of)
within →	inside the limits (*within* my ability)
to →	direction, level

E. As the following newspaper article about a volcano eruption will show you, prepositions are very important when you want to describe something. Fill in the missing prepositions in the paragraph about Krakatoa (a volcano in Indonesia). Use all the prepositions from the language box at least once.

Krakatoa

The islands that form the country of Indonesia are part of the Pacific "ring of fire." Therefore, many important earthquakes and volcano eruptions _____ Earth occur _____ this area. The Krakatoa eruption _____ 1883, for example, is the greatest volcanic eruption that was recorded _____ recent historic times. The volcano had made noise _____ many years before the eruption. The actual Krakatoa event began when a group of islands exploded and most of the visible surface of the volcano disappeared. _____ August 26, 1883, the noises _____ the volcano increased _____ such a level that _____ an area that was 160 km (100 miles) away the houses began to tremble and windows rattled. It is said that the noise became so loud that no one _____ that part of western Java was able to sleep that night. But this was only the beginning.

The next morning _____ about 10 A.M. the eruption reached a climax. As a result of the explosion a gigantic ash cloud rose _____ a height of 80 km (50 miles), and the loud noises could be heard nearly 5,000 km (3,000 miles) away. Ninety minutes later, a gigantic wave, called a *tsunami*, rose _____ a height of 36 m (120 ft) and swept across the Indian Ocean. When this wave hit the coast of Java and Sumatra, it destroyed 295 towns and killed 36,000 people. Many smaller explosions followed, and the amount of ash was so big that it turned daylight into darkness. Three weeks later the dust cloud went _____ Europe and North America. Temperatures throughout the world declined as a result of the explosion.

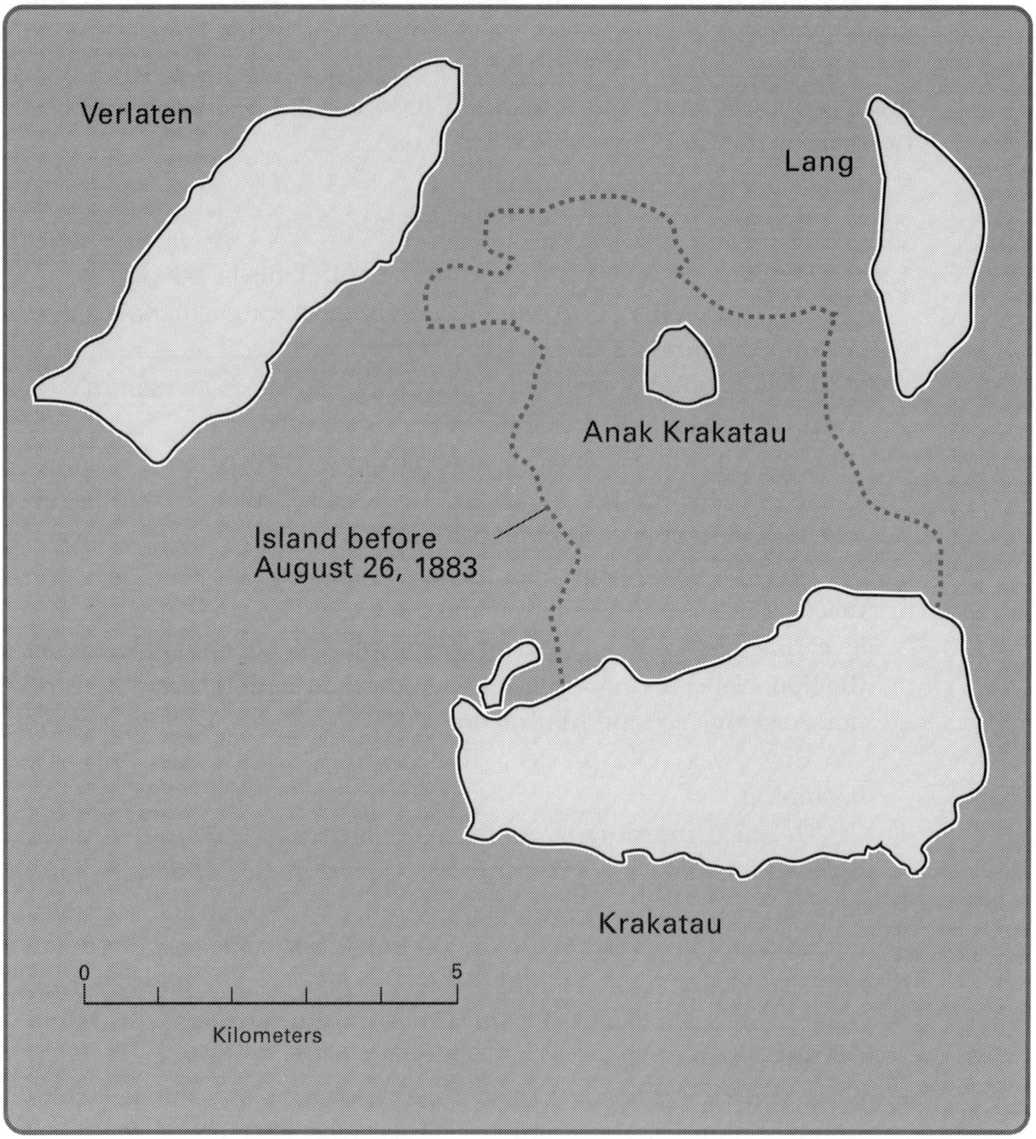
Verlaten
Lang
Anak Krakatau
Island before
August 26, 1883
Krakatau
0
5
Kilometers

F. The newspaper article about the explosion of Krakatoa probably included some new words that you looked up in a dictionary. Let's review briefly all the information you can find about a word when checking an English-English dictionary. Put each number from the dictionary entries on the line next to its corresponding explanation.

7　　3　　6　　　　　2

e·rupt (ĭ-rŭpt′) *v.* **erupted, erupting, erupts.** —*intr.* **1.** To emerge violently from limits or restraint; explode. **2.** To become violently active. **3.** To force out or release suddenly, as something enclosed or pent up: *The geyser erupts periodically.* **4. a.** To pierce the gum. Used of a tooth. **b.** To appear on the skin. Used of a skin blemish. —*tr.* To eject violently (steam, lava, or other confined matter). [Latin *ērumpere* (past participle *ēruptus*), to erupt, to break out, to burst : *ē-*, out, from *ex-* + *rumpere*, to break (see **reup-** in Appendix*).]

— 1

4

5

3　　6

7

e·rup·tion (ĭ-rŭp′shən) *n.* **1.** An act, process, or instance of erupting, especially the discharge of lava from a volcano, or of water or mud from a geyser. **2.** A sudden, often violent outburst. **3. a.** Redness, spotting, or other blemishing of the skin or mucosa, especially as a local manifestation of a general disease. **b.** The passage of a tooth through the gum. —**e·rup′-tive** *adj.* —**e·rup′tive·ly** *adv.*

— 1

2

Copyright © 1996 by Houghton Mifflin Company. Adapted and reproduced from *The American Heritage Dictionary of the English Language,* Third Edition.

__ meaning of the word

__ pronunciation and syllables

__ etymology (history of the word)

__ spelling

__ cross-references

__ inflected forms of the word (how the form of the word changes, usually by changing the ending, to indicate different usages)

__ part of speech

126 · Earthbound

G. Complete the following chart. Some of the words can be found in the passage "Krakatoa" in Activity E. Use a dictionary to look up the words you can't find in the text.

Noun	Verb	Adjective
decline		
	explode	
recording		
		increasing
	begin	
		darkish
destruction		

H. Find the answers to the following questions about the eruption of Krakatoa (Activity E).

1. Did anything before the eruption show that Krakatoa was an active volcano?

2. On what day did the Krakatoa eruption begin?

3. When was the eruption strongest?

4. How far away could people hear the eruption?

5. How high did the ashes fly?

6. What happened in the ocean as a result of the eruption?

7. Why did 36,000 people in Indonesia die?

8. How long did it take the dust clouds to travel to Europe?

9. Did the eruption affect the climate?

I. You are going to write about Mount St. Helens, a volcano in the United States that exploded many years ago. Together with a partner you will have to find out what happened before, during, and after this volcano exploded. When you have all the information, complete the following newspaper article about the eruption.

Mount St. Helens

Volcanoes may lie dormant for many centuries between eruptions.

When they explode, the eruption can be extremely violent. _____

_____

_____

_____

_____

_____

128 · Earthbound

III. Living with Mountains and Volcanoes

A. We studied the life cycle of mountains and volcanoes. Let's think about the functions they have on Earth. With a partner brainstorm about the role of mountains on Earth. Then think about the answers to the following questions.

1. Do you think humans could live without mountains and volcanoes?

2. Why or why not?

3. Do you think mountain areas should be protected?

B. Look at the following picture and describe in your own words what you think it shows.

C. Write two or three paragraphs about the role mountains play for our life on Earth. One group of ideas for one paragraph is given to help you get started. With a classmate try to come up with more ideas before you start writing.

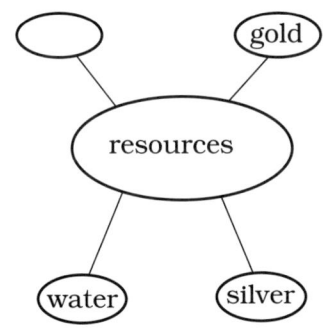

```
        ( )        (gold)
           \      /
          (resources)
           /      \
        (water)  (silver)
```

D. Read the clues and fill in the crossword puzzle.

Across
1. Many people go to mountain areas to practice this type of sport.
2. a different name for the border of a cliff
3. the part of a plant that can break rocks
4. the name for molten rock when it is still inside the earth
5. You are standing on Mount Aconcagua, the highest point in the Western Hemisphere. What country are you in?
6. a name for the area that lies between two mountains
7. Air that has a lot of moisture is called _____.
8. How many centimeters do the Himalayas grow each year?

Down
1. a precious metal that can often be found in mountains
2. When water freezes, it can "become bigger" or _____.
9. the name of the tallest free-standing mountain in the world (The American writer Ernest Hemingway used the name of this mountain in the title of a short story.)
10. the name of a natural force of erosion
11. to wear or rub away
12. an area of ground that is over 300 m (1,000 ft.) high
13. a different name for molten rock that comes to the surface of the earth
14. a mass of ice which moves very slowly down a mountain valley
15. a huge wave that is caused by an earthquake or a volcano eruption
16. The top of a mountain is called a _____.

130 · **Earthbound**

Chapter 7

The Water

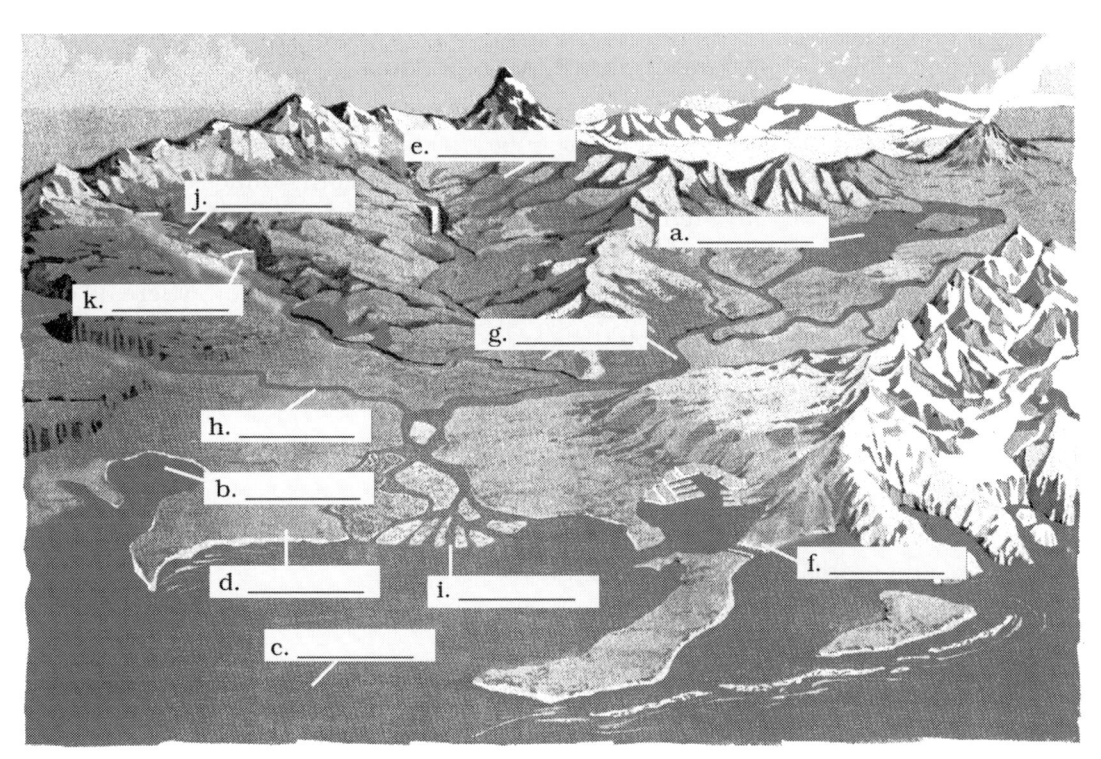

From H. H. Gross, *World Geography* (Englewood Cliffs, NJ: Prentice Hall, 1980).

Look at the picture and write the name for each land/water formation on the blank lines provided. Use the following definition of the word to find the correct object in the picture.

131

bay: a part of a body of water that is surrounded by land

dam: a construction to stop the flow of water and regulate floods

delta: a fan-shaped area of land at the mouth of a river

isthmus: a narrow strip of land that connects two pieces of land

lake: an inland body of freshwater

reservoir: an artificial lake to store water

river: a large stream of water

sea: a large body of saltwater

seashore: the land around a sea

source: the place where a river begins

tributary: a stream or river that flows into a larger river

A Look Behind/A Look Ahead

The discussion of mountains and volcanoes in chapter 6 has shown us that one aspect of the earth cannot be seen in isolation. All the things on Earth are somehow related to each other. Most of all, when you are talking about the land, you also have to talk about water. In fact, 70 percent of the earth's surface is covered by water. This chapter therefore will focus on where all this water comes from, what happens to it, and what role it plays on Earth. We will also review the names of different rivers and bodies of water on Earth.

To the Student

At the end of this chapter, you will be able to

1. name rivers and oceans on the earth;
2. understand the water cycle; and
3. discuss the effects that humans have on the water reservoirs.

Vocabulary Development

Read the following list of important words from chapter 7 (you may have seen some of them in previous chapters). If you already know the word, put a check mark (✓) in the space in front of the word. When you finish the chapter, return to this list. Mark all the new words you learned. Write down additional words that you learned.

__ cycle	__ droplet	__ tiny	__ invisible
__ snowflake	__ melt	__ precipitation	__ reservoir
__ constantly	__ rapidly	__ support	__ transpiration
__ difference	__ groundwater	__ condensation	__ turn into
__ cloud	__ hail	__ vapor	__ crystal
__ freeze	__ soak	__ evaporate	__ condense
__ leave	__ stream	__ source	__ affect
__ dam	__ gorge	__ project	__ capacity
__ impact	__ endangered	__ relocate	__ argue
__ opponents	__ proponents	__ navigation	__ coal

_____   _____   _____   _____

_____   _____   _____   _____

_____   _____   _____   _____

_____   _____   _____   _____

Except for one, we have studied all parts of speech in English (nouns, verbs, adjectives, and prepositions). The beginning of this chapter will help you review what you have learned and it will also present the part of speech we haven't looked at yet. The part of speech we have not talked about in detail is the *adverb*. These words are used to show *how* something is done. They describe the action of the verb.

For example:

   Mountains grow *slowly*.
   The volcano erupted *violently*.

Go through the vocabulary list for this chapter or any of the previous chapters and find five words for each category in the chart. While you are working on the activities in this chapter, add more words to each category. One word may fit in more than one category, but it may also have a very different meaning in each category.

Noun	Verb	Adjective	Adverb	Preposition

The Water · 135

I. Oceans, Rivers, and Lakes of the World

A. Look at the world map and identify the rivers and oceans of the world. If you are not sure, leave the lines blank until you have completed Activity B.

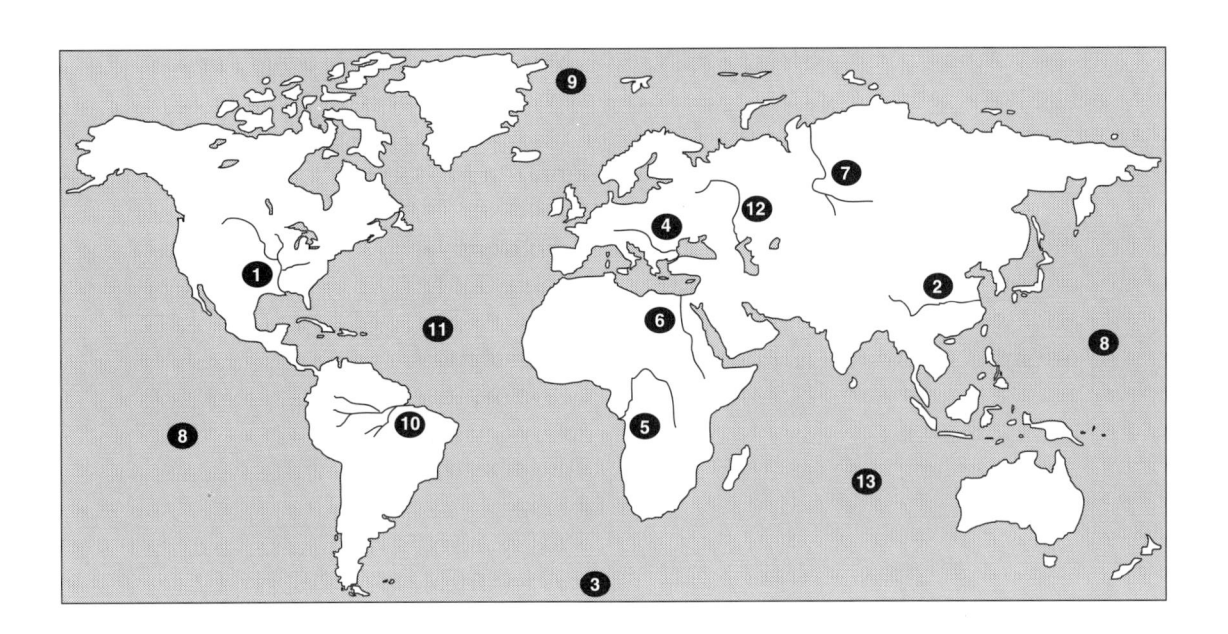

1. _____   6. _____   11. _____

2. _____   7. _____   12. _____

3. _____   8. _____   13. _____

4. _____   9. _____

5. _____   10. _____

B. Listen to the presentation about the oceans and some important rivers on Earth. Fill in the missing numbers in the chart that follows.

Oceans		Rivers	
Name	*Size (sq. miles)*	*Name (continent)*	*Length (miles)*
Pacific Ocean	_____	River Nile (Africa)	_____
Atlantic Ocean	_____	Amazon River (S. America)	_____
Indian Ocean	_____	Yangtze River/ Chang Jiang (Asia)	_____
Antarctic Ocean	_____	Mississippi-Missouri River (N. America)	_____
Arctic Ocean	_____	River Ob-Irtysh (Asia)	_____
		River Congo/ Zaire (Africa)	_____
		Volga (Europe)	_____
		Danube (Europe)	_____

C. How much do you know about water? In groups, answer the following questions about rivers, oceans, and lakes. If you are not sure, just guess and discuss your ideas with a partner.

1. How much of the Earth is water and how much is land (in percentages)?

2. What is the difference between an ocean and a lake?

3. What is the difference between a lake and a river?

4. What is the name of the longest river in South America?

5. What is the name of the longest river in Europe?

6. Which river is longer, the Mississippi (United States) or the Yangtze (China)?

7. Which is the largest (by surface area) freshwater lake on Earth?

8. Which is the deepest lake on Earth?

9. To remember the names of five big lakes in North America, schoolchildren often just remember one word: *HOMES*. What do the five letters in this word stand for?

10. What is the name of the largest ocean in the world?

11. Which ocean is smaller, the Indian or the Antarctic Ocean?

II. The Different Faces of Water

A. Read the riddle. (A riddle is a difficult and amusing question to which one has to guess the answer.) The topic of this riddle has to do with water! Can you guess what this riddle is about? (*Hint:* The word *burgeon* means to *develop* or to *grow*.)

> I have six arms
> And swallow farms.
>
> Millions can
> Become a man.
>
> I cannot fly
> Backwards. I die

138 · **Earthbound**

> When life burgeons.
> My tearful sons
>
> Destroy my shape,
> My perfect shape.
>
> John Fuller

B. On Earth, water is not only found in rivers, oceans, and lakes. Water can take many different faces, or forms. The drawing of the water cycle shows these forms. The following words name important parts in the water cycle. Write the words in their appropriate place around the drawing.

ocean   clouds   plants/trees   Sun   ground

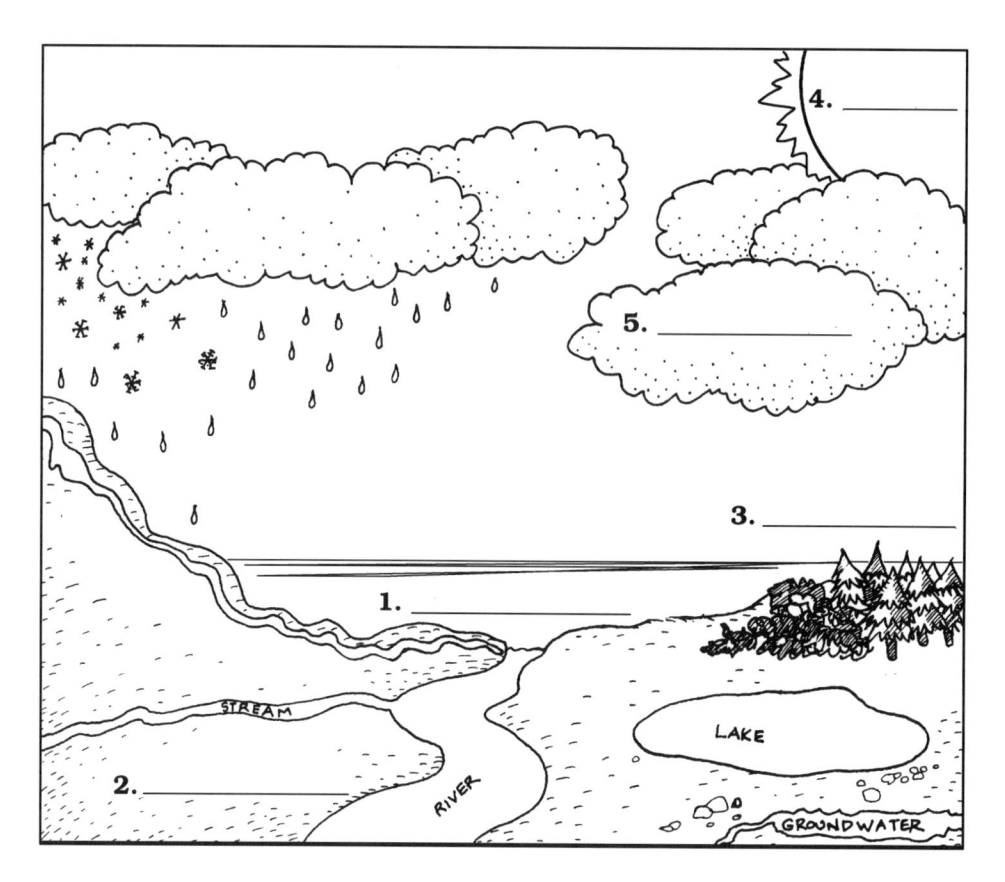

Adapted from A. Deutsch Drutman and S. Klam Zuckerman, *Protecting Our Planet* (Parsippany, NJ: Simon and Schuster Education Group, 1991).

C. Scan the passage "The Water Cycle" as fast as you can and underline all the times that water is mentioned in any form (e.g., include *snow, hail, clouds,* and *water vapor*).

The Water Cycle

1   Water is not only found in rivers and oceans, it is all around
2   us. Water is constantly moving, on land, in the air, and in the sea.
3   This process is called the water cycle. The Sun plays an important
4   role in the water cycle because it heats up the earth's surface and
5   turns some of the liquid water on Earth into water vapor. This
6   change of water into an invisible gas is called evaporation. From the
7   oceans, lakes, and rivers water constantly evaporates into the at-
8   mosphere. Groundwater on Earth may be absorbed by plants and
9   trees and evaporate through their leaves. The process through
10 which water vapor rises from plants is called transpiration.
11   When water vapor in the air cools down, the invisible vapor
12 turns into a liquid or solid that can be seen again. This change from
13 a gas into a liquid or solid is called condensation. The water vapor
14 condenses into water droplets which one can see as clouds. From
15 these clouds in the sky water can fall as rain, snow, or hail.
16   The type of precipitation depends on how cold it is. Ice crystals
17 in the atmosphere grow rapidly into snowflakes when water drop-
18 lets freeze onto them. Most rain outside the tropics is caused by
19 snowflakes which melt as they fall down. On the other hand, if the
20 freezing level (the height at which water freezes when it condenses
21 out of a cloud) is below 1,000 feet (300 m), the ice crystals will not
22 have time to melt before reaching the ground and will fall as snow.
23   About 80 percent of all precipitation on Earth falls into the
24 oceans, lakes, or rivers. The water that doesn't go directly into rivers
25 or oceans either soaks into the ground (it is then called ground-
26 water) or stays on the surface of the earth (it is then called surface
27 runoff). As water evaporates from the surface of the earth and the
28 oceans, the cycle starts over.

D. Read the sentences from "The Water Cycle" and select the meaning that the italicized word has in the given sentence. In some cases, all three answers are possible definitions for this word. Decide which one fits the given context best.

1. The *cycle* of the seasons is similar all over the Northern Hemisphere.

    a. bicycle
    b. period
    c. order

2. A cloud is a mass of *vapor* in the sky.

    a. a product of imagination
    b. a high-flying aircraft in the air
    c. a gaslike form of a liquid

3. Drinking water usually comes from *groundwater*, rivers, or lakes.

    a. a piece of empty land
    b. water below the earth's surface
    c. water on top of the land

4. When water turns into vapor it *becomes invisible*.

    a. cannot be seen
    b. becomes strong
    c. is not recorded

5. Some types of soil, for example sand, can *absorb* more water than others.

    a. take out
    b. suck in
    c. take over

6. It has rained a lot during the last couple of weeks. The fields are *soaked*.

    a. washed well
    b. thoroughly wet
    c. taking a bath

7. When hot steam cools down, it *condenses* and forms water drops.

    a. has a shortened form
    b. becomes liquid
    c. has a thickened form

8. Water *freezes* at a temperature of 0°C.

   a. doesn't work properly
   b. hardens into ice
   c. is preserved and cold

9. The *hail* damaged a lot of houses and cars in the area.

   a. frozen raindrops
   b. violent things
   c. to call out to someone

E. Based on the reading passage "The Water Cycle" write on the blank line next to each arrow the word for the process it represents.

evaporation   transpiration
condensation   precipitation   surface runoff

Adapted from A. Deutsch Drutman and S. Klam Zuckerman, *Protecting Our Planet* (Parsippany, NJ: Simon and Schuster Education Group, 1991).

F. Make a list of all the "forms" of water discussed in "The Water Cycle" and say what can happen to them.

Example:

    cloud: float   form   rise

III. Living with Water

A. Discuss the following questions in groups.

1. Why have early civilizations always begun near rivers or bodies of water?

2. How do humans use water? How much water do you think you need each day?

3. How do humans affect the water cycle?

4. Can you think of problems that humans create with respect to water reservoirs?

B. In the following picture all the people and animals are doing different things in or by the water. Look at the following sentences about the picture. Which of the two sentences gives a better description of the little boy in the middle of the picture?

1. The boy is swimming in the water.
2. The boy swims very well.

The Water · 143

Adapted from J. Fein, R. Gerber, and P. Wilson, *The Geography Teacher's Guide to the Classroom*. (South Melbourne, Victoria: Macmillan Education Australia, 1984).

> *Present Progressive*
>
> The present progressive is used for an activity that is in progress at the time the speaker is saying the sentence. In other words, the event began in the past, is going on right now, and will probably continue into the future.
>
> To form the present progressive you use
>
> a form of *to be* (am, are, is) + verb + -ing
>
> The man *is* swimm*ing* in the river.
>
> The fish *are* swimm*ing* in the river.

C. Here is a copy of the river scene in Activity B. There are ten differences in this copy of the picture. Get together with a partner. One of you should look at this picture. The other should look at the picture in Activity B. Describe the picture you are looking at to your partner. Without looking at both pictures, you two must find the differences. Make sure you use the correct form of the verbs!

144 · **Earthbound**

Adapted from J. Fein, R. Gerber, and P. Wilson, *The Geography Teacher's Guide to the Classroom*. (South Melbourne, Victoria: Macmillan Education Australia, 1984).

D. Answer the questions about the picture in Activity B.

1. Would you like to be at the beach shown in the picture? Why or why not?

2. Can you think of problems that the animals or the people there may have?

3. If there are any problems, what can be done to solve them?

E. The discussion of the river scene has shown that water can be used in many different ways. It may also have shown that there are some areas in the world that don't have a lot of water or that experience water shortages. These people are searching for ways to ease the water crisis. You can find out about it if you crack the code that is shown here. For many years, semaphore flags, held in different positions, have been a way to send messages. Can you decode the messages in semaphore on page 146 to discover some water pollution solutions?

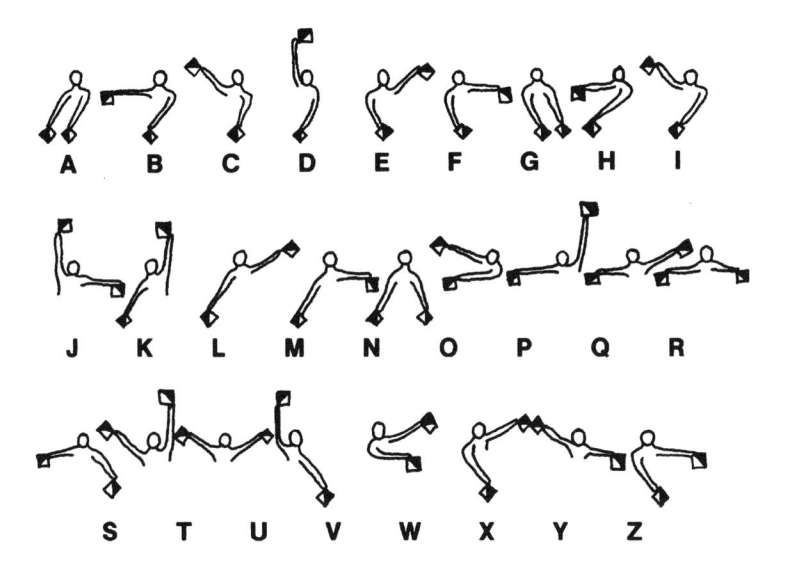

1. _____

2. _____

3. _____

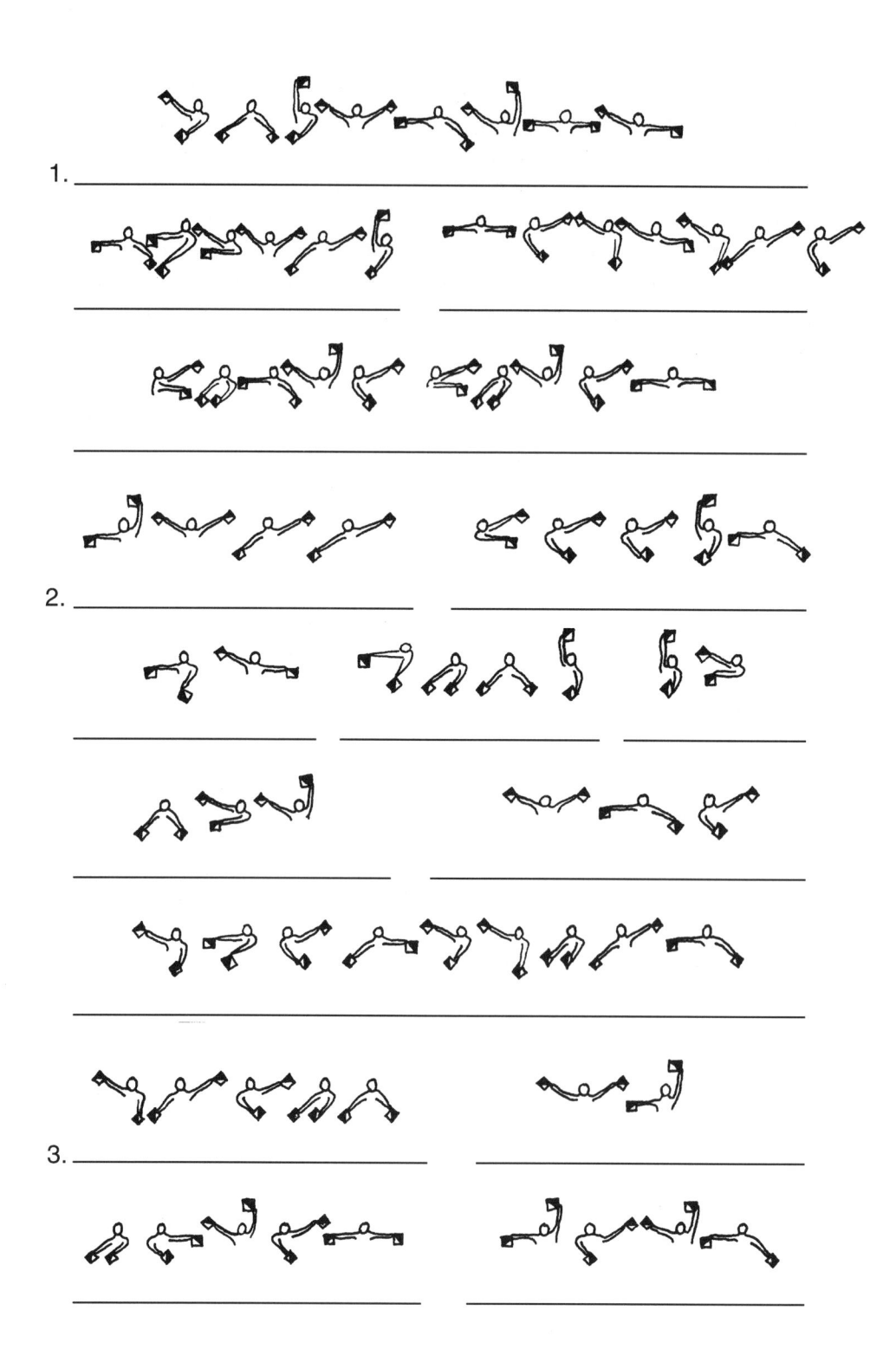

From A. Deutsch Drutman and S. Klam Zuckerman, *Protecting Our Planet* (Parsippany, NJ: Simon and Schuster Education Group, 1991).

IV. Water and Humans

A. Before you look at the case study in this section, you will practice guessing the meanings of unfamiliar vocabulary words.

Guessing Vocabulary from Context

When you are reading something in English, there may be some vocabulary words that you don't understand. It is not always necessary to look up these words in a dictionary. You can actually guess the meanings of these words by looking at the surrounding context. For example:

A dam in the Yangtze River can _____ a lot of electricity.

In this sentence, we know that the missing word, or the word we don't know, is a verb that has to follow the auxiliary *can*. We can also guess that the word must have the meaning of *make, produce,* or *generate,* because this is something that a dam can do with electricity. Try this strategy and never get discouraged if a sentence contains an unfamiliar word.

Read the following sentences and try to guess the meaning of the italicized words based on the context. Write your definition under the sentence. Then check the dictionary to see if you are right.

1. One can produce electricity by using wind or the Sun. These *renewable* resources of energy are better than coal or oil because they are clean and not limited.

2. Most rivers begin in the mountains. When they flow from their source in the mountains to their *mouth* at the ocean, they often get polluted.

3. Some big rivers like the Yangtze in China have cut deep *gorges* into the mountains.

4. A dam in a river uses the river's supply of water to produce *hydroelectric* power.

5. There are different ways for a government to *promote* economic development. For example, it can build new roads and provide cheap electricity for new companies.

6. Every spring when the snow melts in the mountains, the river carries a lot of water and *floods* the valley.

7. Before the flow of water in the Yangtze River can be stopped and the valley can be flooded, the Chinese government will *relocate* 1.4 million people who still live there.

B. We have looked at different ways in which humans can use water. The following case study describes a project that has an effect on water. Look at the title of the reading passage, the pictures, and the headings. Based on that information, what do you predict this reading to be about? Write down any words or phrases in the following space that represent what the text will be about.

C. Read the passage.

The Three Gorges Project: Dammed If They Do?

Taming the Wild River

The Yangtze Kiang, also called Chang Jiang or "long river" in Chinese, is the third longest river in the world and the longest, most important, river in China. It runs for about 3,915 miles (6,300 km) across China. Halfway between its source in Tibet and the fertile delta at its mouth in Shanghai, the river flows through a canyon area that is commonly known as the Three Gorges. This area may soon become the site of the world's largest hydroelectric dam. The dam, scheduled to be completed by the year 2009, will be 1.2 miles (1,900 m) long and about 610 feet high (185 m). The water in its reservoir will drive turbines with a generating capacity of almost 18,000 megawatts. This is eight times that of the Aswan Dam on the Nile, four times greater than any power station in Europe, and 50 percent more than the world's largest existing hydroelectric dam, Itaipu in Paraguay.

Estimates of the project's cost range between $17 billion and $30 billion. Most of it will be provided by the Chinese government, but about $8 billion is needed in foreign investment. Governments in different countries all over the world and organizations such as the World Bank are discussing the funding for this project.

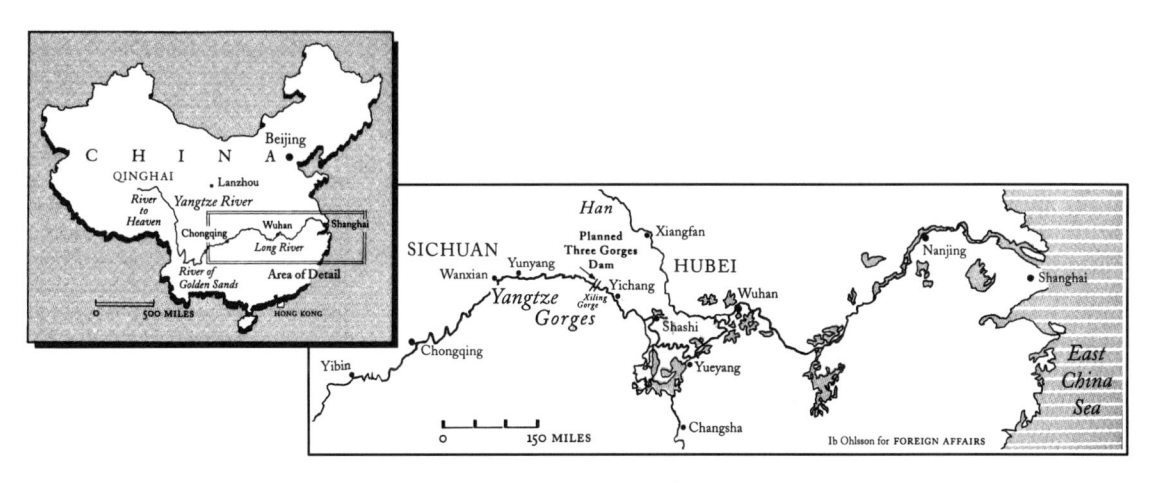

An Important Project for the Country

It will be very difficult for the rapidly growing nation of 1.2 billion people, all of whom would like refrigerators and other conveniences, to promote economic development without having some negative impact on the environment. The proponents of the dam, or people that support it, argue that Three Gorges is the best way to provide clean energy for China. Currently China uses coal to supply 75 percent of the country's energy needs, and coal causes a lot more pollution than hydroelectric power created by a dam. In fact, the burning of coal is a major source of pollution in the country, and it has helped to make pulmonary disease the nation's leading cause of death. The burning of coal also contributes considerably to acid rain and the greenhouse effect. These environmental problems affect not only China but the whole world.

Besides reducing China's heavy reliance on coal, Three Gorges will also help in the overall development of the region. First, the dam will provide critically needed energy for China's inland central-southern region. Second, it will bring energy for industrialization and reduce the risk of floods, thus making the area more attractive for businesses. Third, the dam will improve navigation along the Yangtze and make the area more accessible for further development.

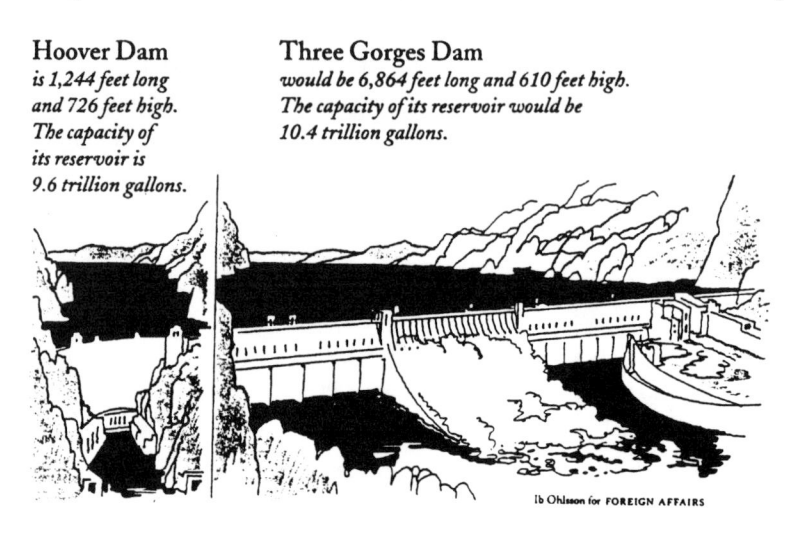

Hoover Dam
is 1,244 feet long and 726 feet high. The capacity of its reservoir is 9.6 trillion gallons.

Three Gorges Dam
would be 6,864 feet long and 610 feet high. The capacity of its reservoir would be 10.4 trillion gallons.

Ib Ohlsson for FOREIGN AFFAIRS

Incalculable Environmental Costs

Opponents of the project, on the other hand, argue that the natural beauty of the area will be destroyed. In addition, the dam will also have a negative effect on the people and different animals living in the area. First, 1.4 million people will have to be relocated before the completion of this project. About 13 cities and hundreds of villages as well as 115,000 acres of rich land along the river basin will be covered with water. Second, the water reservoir that will stretch 385 miles up the Yangtze River will flood such important cultural sites as ancient temples and archaeological treasures. Third, animals like the Yangtze River alligator and sturgeon (a giant fish that dates back to the age of the dinosaur and can only be found in this river), the freshwater dolphin (there are only 200 animals left), the cloud leopard, and the Siberian white crane might become endangered or extinct.

The Future of the Dam

Supporters of the Three Gorges argue that the project could save large numbers of people from periodic floods, generate electricity from a renewable resource, and improve navigation. Many Chinese people and international environmentalists and foreign governments do not agree. Because construction has begun on the dam, their voices may not be heard.

<small>This text is adapted from an article that originally appeared in *Foreign Affairs* called "Ecological Roulette: Damming the Yangtze" by Audrey R. Topping, Sept/Oct 95. Copyright 1995 by the Council on Foreign Relations, Inc.</small>

D. Scan the passages "The Three Gorges Project" and match the following arguments with the paragraph they belong to. Then fill out the blank chart. In the first column, put the letters of the arguments that *support* the construction of the dam (*pro* arguments). In the second column, put the letters of the arguments that *do not support* the construction of the dam (*con* arguments).

		Paragraph #
a.	The dam will prevent floods.	___
b.	Use of hydroelectric power will avoid more air pollution.	___
c.	The price of the dam is not certain yet.	___
d.	Some animals will be endangered.	___
e.	The dam will improve economic growth in the area.	___
f.	People will have to leave the area where the dam will be.	___

Pros	Cons

E. Answer the following questions about the passage "The Three Gorges Project."

1. What is the Chinese name for the Yangtze River and what does the name mean in English?

2. In which city does the Yangtze River empty into the ocean?

3. Where in China is the dam located and when is the project scheduled to be completed?

4. Do we know how much the Three Gorges project is going to cost?

5. How much of China's energy is currently supplied by coal?

6. Which is a cleaner source of energy, hydroelectric power or coal?

7. Describe two ways in which the dam can help China.

8. Describe two ways in which the dam can harm China.

F. The arguments for the construction of the dam are summarized in the following chart. After the chart, there is a list of arguments against the project. Match these counterarguments to the given arguments by writing a, b, and c in their appropriate places in the chart.

Arguments for construction	Arguments against construction
1. Three Gorges will provide clean energy for China. Today about 180 million Chinese people live without electricity. In the southwestern part of the country, the energy available per person is roughly 1 percent of that in the United States. To satisfy the needs of the people, the dam can produce almost the equivalent of ten nuclear power plants.	
2. The construction of a dam will prevent the periodic flooding that often occurs in the areas surrounding the river bed. In this century alone 500,000 people have died as a result of these floods. If a dam is constructed and the flow of the water is changed, the floods can be better controlled.	
3. Three Gorges would raise the water level by about 500 feet. This will improve river navigation and enable 10,000 ton ships to go up the gorges to Chongqing (currently only small ships can travel on the river). The dam would increase capacity for shipping fivefold and decrease shipping costs by about 35 percent. It would also make the area more accessible and lead to industrial development, providing jobs for the people.	

a. Even though shipping costs will be reduced, the use of 10,000 ton ships on the river would make it necessary to build expensive bridges and giant locks in other parts of the river. More traffic on the Yangtze and more industrial development in the area will lead to more pollution and further endanger the environment.

b. American engineers say that the construction of the dam will change the course of the Yangtze River and actually increase the risk of floods. Most importantly, if a dam of this size breaks (due to landslides, earthquakes, or construction problems), between 270,000 and 400,000 cubic yards of water per second would roar downstream, covering dozens of towns and threatening the lives of 10,000,000 people.

c. In the future, due to the fast economic growth of the country, China will probably need an additional 17,000 megawatts of electrical generating capacity each year. So, overall, the dam will only generate 10 percent of the electrical capacity China will need in the future, and there are other sources of clean energy that could be developed.

G. Using the summary of the arguments for and against the construction of the dam (*pro* and *con*), decide in groups which alternative you support and why.

H. Look at the following letters about the Three Gorges project. Who do you think these letters are intended for? What do you think the writer wants to achieve with the letters?

January 22, 19--

Dear Joe,

How are you? I miss you and your family. I also miss living in the United States! My hometown here in China is facing a difficult time. Some people want to build a dam called the Three Gorges. This dam will be five times bigger than the Hoover Dam! If they build it, my family will have to move because this area will be underwater. Can you believe it? There is no way I am just gonna watch this happen. The government has already started building the dam, but some people are trying to stop them and I will definitely join the group. I'll let you know what happens. Say hello to your family and our friends. Write soon.

Quibao

January 25, 19--

Quibao Pan
101 Village Trade Building
23 Haidian Road
Beijing 100015 PRC

James D. Wolfensohn, President
World Bank
1818 H Street NW
Washington, DC 20433

Dear President Wolfensohn,

I am a resident of the town of Wanxian in the southern part of China. Since the life of my family will be severely affected by the construction of the Three Gorges Dam in this area, I would like to ask you to refrain from supporting this project.

As you know, the construction of the dam will lead to the flooding of my hometown. However, my family has been farming in this area for more than 100 years and we have no other means of supporting ourselves. The Chinese government has said that they will move us to a new area in the mountains, but we won't be able to farm there. We don't know any other lifestyle, so we don't know how we will survive.

People who support this dam say that it will give the Chinese people the energy we will need for the future. However, I have heard that the dam will only supply 10% of that energy. China could develop other clean sources of energy, like solar energy, that won't have such a horrible impact on so many Chinese people.

I appreciate your time and know you will do what is best for the people of China.

Sincerely,

Quibao Pan

Quibao Pan

Audience and Purpose

When you write something it is important to think about the people who will read what you have written (the audience) and the reason for writing (the purpose). The styles of the two letters on the Three Gorges reflect the differences in audience and purpose.

When you know your audience it is easier to achieve your goal of communication. Your audience will determine what you say and how you say it. You must consider what your audience knows and doesn't know. Finally, your relationship with the reader influences the content, the organization, the sentence structure, and the words you use in writing.

The second aspect that will influence your writing is the purpose. Before you start writing, you probably know what you want the readers to do when they are finished reading. For example, you may want to ask for information or entertain, persuade, or describe something to the reader.

I. How are samples A and B different? Make specific comments on the differences in content, organization, grammar, and word choice.

J. Write a letter to the World Bank or some other international institution involved in funding the project and argue for or against its support of the project. You can write from the perspective of one of the following people.

1. yourself
2. a Chinese government official
3. the head of the environmental organization "Water Is Beautiful"
4. the president of a construction company that will be working on the dam

5. other: _____

References

Burton, Sandra. "Taming the River Wild." *Time,* December 19, 1994, 62–64.

Pearce, Fred. "Return of the Giant Dams." *World Press Review,* May 1995, 37–38.

Sullivan, Lawrence R. "The Three Gorges Project: Dammed If They Do?" *Current History,* September 1995, 266–69.

Topping, Audrey R. "Ecological Roulette: Damming the Yangtze." *Foreign Affairs,* September/October 1995, 132–46.

Chapter 8

Weather and Climate

From the *State News*, January 11, 1995, Volume 90, no. 91.

What do the pictures show?
What do you think is the difference between weather and climate?

A Look Behind/A Look Ahead

Both aspects of physical geography, land and water, come together in the final chapter of this book. This chapter will focus on weather and climate on Earth. Both weather and climate are affected by the distribution of land and water. Weather and climate, on the other hand, have a tremendous effect on how and where human beings live. The weather affects our habits and lifestyles and in many cultures the weather is talked about a lot and blamed for many things. This chapter looks at some general aspects of weather and climate on Earth and how they affect us. The chapter begins with some basic concepts of weather phenomena.

To the Student

After completing this chapter, you will be able to

1. describe different weather phenomena;
2. understand different weather and climate patterns; and
3. discuss the effects that climate has on lifestyles.

Vocabulary Development

Read the following list of important words from chapter 8 (you may have seen some of them in previous chapters). If you already know the word, put a check mark (✓) in the space behind the word. When you finish the chapter, return to this list. Mark all the new words you learned. Write down additional words that you learned.

__ drizzle	__ storm	__ awful	__ tornado
__ flood	__ fog	__ cloudy	__ weather
__ degrees	__ hurricane	__ forecast	__ precipitation
__ breath	__ expect	__ to be like	__ frequency
__ record	__ unpleasant	__ sunny	__ pond
__ solid	__ sympathetic	__ shrivel	__ sweat
__ stir	__ sprout	__ mighty	__ chill
__ mist	__ prediction	__ magic	__ preconceived

_____   _____   _____   _____

_____   _____   _____   _____

_____   _____   _____   _____

_____   _____   _____   _____

Many words in English begin with the same syllable or end in the same syllable or sound. These parts of a word are called prefixes or suffixes. They can give information about the meaning of a word and about the part of speech it belongs to.

Examples:

        pleasant   unpleasant
        like   dislike

The prefixes *un-* and *dis-* give a word the opposite meaning.

        cloud   cloudy
        friend   friendly

The suffixes *-y* and *-ly* can be added to some nouns. They turn the noun into an adjective.

Find words in this and previous chapters that have suffixes and prefixes. Then discuss their meanings with your classmates.

I. Weather Reports

A. Discuss the following questions with a partner. Try to come up with as many answers as possible.

1. How can you find out what the weather will be like tomorrow or next week?

2. Why is it important to know what the weather will be like?

162 · Earthbound

3. Which groups of people especially need to watch the weather and why?

B. Do people in your country talk a lot about the weather? In the United States "the weather" is a very popular topic when people first meet. The following adjectives are all used to describe the weather. Sort the adjectives according to whatever category you can come up with.

snowy   drizzling   rainy   nice   stormy   windy
   sunny   cloudy   foggy   humid   hot
beautiful   awful   cool   warm   cold   freezing

C. If you look at the adjectives in Activity B, you will see that some of them end in -y. Write all adjectives ending in -y on the blank lines. Write the corresponding noun next to the adjective. Can you come up with a rule for the formation of these weather adjectives?

Adjective   *Noun*

_____   _____

_____   _____

_____   _____

_____   _____

_____   _____

_____   _____

Rule: _____

_____

Weather and Climate · 163

D. Imagine you just received "today's" weather report in the *Lansing State Journal*. Scan the report on page 165 for the following information.

1. What is "today's" date?

2. What will the weather in Lansing be like in two days from "today?"

3. What will the weather in Traverse City be like "today"?

4. How high are the waves on Lake Superior going to be "today"?

5. What type of weather can people who live on the Upper Peninsula (UP) expect?

6. When will you be able to observe a new moon?

7. In what year was the record high/low for June 5?

8. What do the following symbols from weather maps stand for?

   a

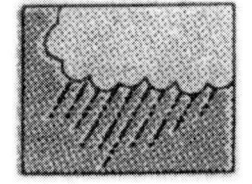

   b

   c

9. Is there a number I can call if I need more information about the weather? Is the call free?

10. Would you like being in the Twin Cities (St. Paul and Minneapolis in Minnesota) today?

11. Which parts of the United States are going to see rain today?

12. What was the weather like in Frankfurt, Montreal, Seoul, and Tokyo yesterday? Which of these cities was the hottest? Can you guess what the abbreviations *clr* and *cdy* stand for?

Sunday, June 6, 1993   6B

Weather

Lansing forecast
Today: Partly cloudy skies expected, high in the mid- to upper 70s. Chance of rain tonight, low 55 to 60.

Local five-day forecast

Today	Monday	Tuesday	Wednesday	Thursday
Partly cloudy	Rain	Chance of rain	Chance of rain	Partly cloudy
Hi: 78 Lo: 57	Hi: 75 Lo: 58	Hi: 82 Lo: 59	Hi: 80 Lo: 57	Hi: 75 Lo: 53

Lower Peninsula forecast
Today: Partly cloudy, highs 75 to 80. Chance of rain tonight, lows 50 to 60. Rain likely on Monday, highs in the low to mid-70s.
Tuesday: 75-85/60s/chance of rain
Wednesday: 75-85/60s/chance of rain
Thursday: 70s/50s/partly cloudy

Upper Peninsula forecast
Today: Chance of rain, highs in the low to mid-70s. Showers likely tonight, lows 50 to 55. Rain on Monday, highs 60 to 70.
Tuesday: 65-70/50s/chance of rain
Wednesday: 65-70/50s/chance of rain
Thursday: 65-70/45-50/partly cloudy

Yesterday's local almanac
High: 65 Low: 47
Record high/low: 96 in 1925; 27 in 1869.
State high/low: Traverse City: 68; Marquette: 41.
Nation high/low: Presidio, Texas: 107; Truckee, Calif.: 29.
Precipitation: Saturday, .39 inch; month, .71 inch; year, 13.08 inches; June normal, 2.61 inches
Wind speed: 23 mph from the N at 6:53 a.m.

Today's skywatch
Sunrise: 6:01 a.m.; Sunset: 9:13 p.m.;
Moonrise: 11:09 p.m.; Moonset: 8:01 a.m.

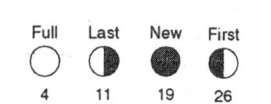

Full 4 | Last 11 | New 19 | First 26

Today's forecast
- Marquette 72/53
- Sault Ste. Marie 75/50
- Escanaba 75/53
- Traverse City 78/55
- Saginaw 79/57
- Grand Rapids 78/57
- Lansing 78/57
- Kalamazoo 77/56
- Detroit 78/57

80s / 70s / 60s / 50s / 40s / 30s

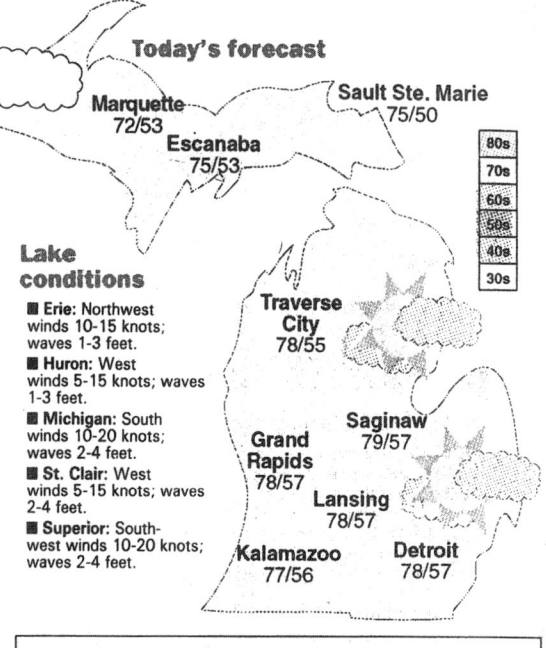

Lake conditions
- **Erie:** Northwest winds 10-15 knots; waves 1-3 feet.
- **Huron:** West winds 5-15 knots; waves 1-3 feet.
- **Michigan:** South winds 10-20 knots; waves 2-4 feet.
- **St. Clair:** West winds 5-15 knots; waves 2-4 feet.
- **Superior:** Southwest winds 10-20 knots; waves 2-4 feet.

Today's travel planner
Chicago: Cloudy; 75, 47.
Cleveland: Cloudy; 73, 49.
Detroit: Sunny; 78, 57.
L.A.: Rain; 73, 59.
Twin Cities: Rain; 71, 55.
New York: Cloudy; 75, 57.
Orlando: Cloudy; 92, 71.
Pittsburgh: Cloudy; 75, 50.
Washington, D.C.: Cloudy; 79, 56.

Today's national forecast
The Accu-Weather® forecast for noon, Sunday, June 6.

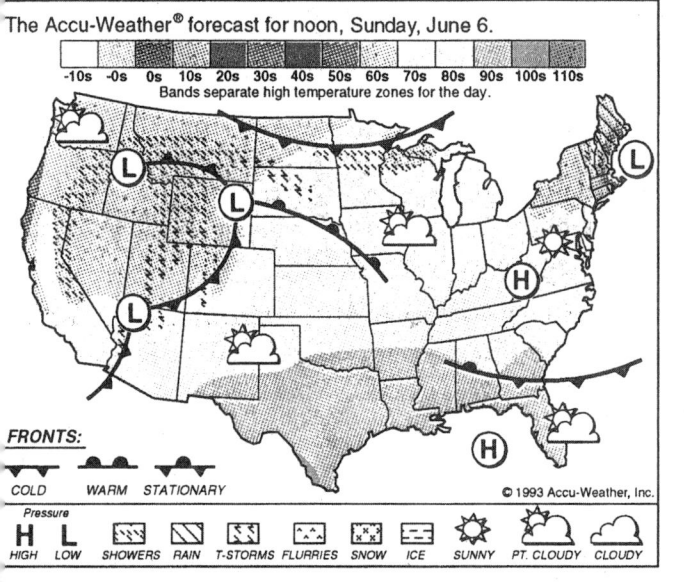

-10s -0s 0s 10s 20s 30s 40s 50s 60s 70s 80s 90s 100s 110s
Bands separate high temperature zones for the day.

FRONTS: COLD WARM STATIONARY

Pressure: H HIGH L LOW SHOWERS RAIN T-STORMS FLURRIES SNOW ICE SUNNY PT. CLOUDY CLOUDY

© 1993 Accu-Weather, Inc.

Yesterday's conditions

Nation

City	Hi	Lo	Pr	Cond	City	Hi	Lo	Pr	Cond
Albany,N.Y.	60	40	.33	cdy	Louisville	66	56	.86	cdy
Anchorage	66	43		cdy	Memphis	77	62		cdy
Atlanta	90	73		clr	Miami Beach	86	76	.04	rn
Atlantic City	67	58	.08	clr	Milwaukee	76	45	.78	cdy
Austin	92	73		cdy	Mpls-St Paul	74	46		cdy
Baltimore	74	57	.19	cdy	New Orleans	91	68		cdy
Boston	68	52	.05	cdy	New York City	64	57	.15	clr
Buffalo	58	51	1.7	cdy	Oklahoma City	80	53		cdy
Charlotte,N.C.	92	74		clr	Philadelphia	66	59	.01	clr
Cheyenne	67	46		rn	Phoenix	96	71		cdy
Chicago	71	46	.08	cdy	Pittsburgh	65	54	.01	cdy
Cincinnati	64	56	.53	cdy	Portland,Ore.	69	57	.13	cdy
Columbia,S.C.	93	71		clr	Providence	69	48	.01	cdy
Dallas	93	71		cdy	Raleigh	92	63	.13	clr
Dayton	64	52	.01	cdy	Rapid City	74	44	.07	rn
Denver	82	47		clr	Reno	52	41	.16	cdy
El Paso	97	61		clr	Richmond	87	60	.79	clr
Evansville	70	55	.02	cdy	St Louis	71	48		cdy
Fairbanks	86	52		rn	Salt Lake City	69	54	.01	rn
Fargo	75	46		rn	San Antonio	92	76		cdy
Flagstaff	68	37		cdy	San Diego	68	57	.34	cdy
Helena	63	49	.02	cdy	San Francisco	65	53		clr
Honolulu	85	73		clr	Sioux Falls	71	44		rn
Houston	90	75		cdy	Tallahassee	96	70		cdy
Indianapolis	69	51		cdy	Tampa	89	71		cdy
Jackson,Miss.	92	73		clr	Topeka	68	43		rn
Jacksonville	94	66		cdy	Tucson	97	61		cdy
Kansas City	70	44		rn	Tulsa	78	53		cdy
Las Vegas	75	59		cdy	Wshngtn,D.C.	81	60	.32	clr
Little Rock	74	60		cdy	Wichita	75	49		rn
Los Angeles	68	59	.76	clr	Wilmington	69	59		cdy

World

City	Hi	Lo	Cond	City	Hi	Lo	Cond	City	Hi	Lo	Cond
Amsterdam	75	54	clr	London	73	57	clr	Sapporo	68	52	cdy
Brussels	75	52	clr	Mexico City	83	59	cdy	Seoul	79	57	clr
Frankfurt	72	57	clr	Montreal	65	47	clr	Sydney	57	50	rn
Geneva	71	46	clr	Paris	77	55	clr	Tokyo	73	64	cdy
Hong Kong	84	82	cdy	Rome	77	57	clr	Toronto	64	42	cdy
Jerusalem	82	63	clr	San Juan	93	77	cdy	Warsaw	75	57	cdy

Weather & travel hotline
1-900-555-0000
Then press 1

Cost: 95 cents a minute.
Touch-tone phone: Dial the number and wait for instructions, or immediately press 1. Punch in area code for the U.S. city you want; for Lansing area weather information, that's 517. You can choose weather or road conditions.
Pulse phone: Call on pulse, then switch to tone after dialing.
Rotary phone: Only sports results available.

From the *Lansing State Journal*. Sunday, June 6, 1993. Page 6B.

E. Look at question 2 in Activity D. Is that question talking about today's weather? Weather reports often predict the weather for the next day or week. Since they are talking about events in the future, you will often see the *future tense* in weather reports.

Future Tense

The forms of *be going to* and *will* are used to say that something is taking place in the future. They usually express the same meaning when they are used to make *predictions* about the future.

It *is going to* rain tomorrow.
It *will* rain tomorrow.

Usually a form of *be going to* is used to express a *preconceived plan.*

I *am going to* shovel snow this afternoon.

Usually the auxiliary *will* is used to express *willingness* to do something.

I'll / I will help you shovel the snow.

F. Next weekend, you and your partner are planning to drive from Chicago to Madison, Wisconsin, to visit a friend. Your teacher will give each of you a different part of the weather forecast for Chicago for that next weekend. Ask your partner for the information that you are missing in your forecast. Then make plans about when you should drive and why.
Phrases you can use:

Is it going to . . . ?
Will it . . . ?
What is . . . going to be like on the weekend?

II. Seasons and Climate

A. The following story was told by the Seneca tribe of Native Americans. They used to live in the area east of the Mississippi. The story is related to the topic of this chapter, but the title of the story was left out. Read each paragraph and then answer the questions following the paragraph. Do not continue reading until you have answered the questions for each paragraph. Sometimes you will have to guess what the answer is! Ignore the italicized words for now.

Paragraph 1

When the world was new, long ago, an old man was wandering around. *This* old man had long, white hair, and wherever he stepped the ground grew hard as stone. When *he* breathed the rivers stopped flowing and the ponds became solid. The birds and animals fled before *him*, and plants dried up and died as leaves shriveled and fell from the trees.

1. Who or what is the old man?

2. Which adjectives do you think characterize the old man best? Circle the two adjectives that you think describe him best.

   angry   intelligent   frustrated   frightened
   warm   friendly   cold   sympathetic

Paragraph 2

Finally this old man found a place where he could set up his lodge. *He* made the walls of ice and covered *it* over with snow. He sat inside his lodge in front of a fire that gave off no heat, though a strange flickering light came from *it*. His only friend was the North Wind, who sat beside the fire with him and laughed as they spoke of things *they* did to make the world a cold, hard place. They sat and smoked their pipes through the long, white nights.

3. Who is the old man's only friend?

4. Why are the nights described as long and white?

Story from *Keepers of the Earth: Native American Stories and Environmental Activities for Children* © by Michael J. Caduto and Joseph Bruchac. With permission of the publisher, Fulcrum Publishing, Inc. Golden, Colorado 80401 (800) 992-2908.

168 · Earthbound

Paragraphs 3–5

One morning, though, as the two dozed by their fire, *they* felt that something was wrong. The air was harder to breathe, and when they looked outside, they saw strange things happening. The snowdrifts were growing smaller. Cracks were forming in the ice on the ponds.

"Hey!" said the North Wind. "I can stay no longer." *He* went out of the lodge and flew through the air toward the north, not stopping until he again reached a place where snow and ice were deep and there was no warmth. But the old man did not stir. *He* knew his magic was strong. He had built his lodge to last.

Now, there came a knocking at his door. Someone was striking against the ice so hard that pieces were falling away from *his* blows.

5. Why does the north wind leave?

6. Who do you think is at the door?

Paragraph 6

"Go away!" the old man shouted. "No one can enter my lodge." Even as *he* said *it,* the door of the lodge broke and fell to the ground. A young man with a smile on his face stood there. Without a word *he* stepped into the lodge and sat on the other side of the fire from the old man. He held a green stick in his hand and with *it* he stirred the fire. As he stirred the fire *it* began to grow warm. The old man felt sweat begin to run down his face.

7. What was the young man holding in his hand when he came into the lodge?

8. What is the color of the object he was holding? Can you explain why the Seneca chose this color for it?

Paragraphs 7 and 8

"Who are you?" said the old man. "Why have you broken my door? No one can come in here but my friend, the North Wind. If you do not leave, I will freeze you with my breath." Then the old man tried to blow *his* chilly breath at the young stranger, but only a thin mist came from *his* lips. The young man laughed. "Old man," he said, "let me stay here and warm myself by your fire."

The old man grew angry. "I am the one who makes the birds and the animals flee. Wherever I step the ground turns into flint. I make the snow and ice. I am mightier than you." As he spoke, though, the old man felt more sweat run off his brow, and the young man continued to smile.

9. Why is the old man sweating?

10. Why is the old man angry?

Paragraph 9

"Listen," the stranger said, "I am young and strong. You cannot frighten me. Surely you know who I am. Do you not feel how warm my breath is? Wherever I breathe the plants grow and the flowers bloom. Where I step the grasses sprout and snow melts away. The birds and animals come to me. See how long my hair is? Your hair is falling out now, old man. Wherever I travel I bring the sunshine and you cannot stay. Do you not know me, old man? Do you not hear my companion, the fawn? *She* is the South Wind. She is blowing on your lodge. It is *your* time to leave."

11. Do you think that the young man's comment about the hair has a special meaning? What does it symbolize?

12. Who or what is the fawn?

170 · Earthbound

Paragraph 10

The old man opened his mouth to speak, but no words came out. He grew smaller and smaller and the sweat poured from his brow as he melted away. Then he was gone. The walls of his lodge of ice and snow fell in. Where his cold fire had burned, white flowers now bloomed. Once again, the young man had defeated the old man.

13. Write down two adjectives that you think describe the young man and two adjectives for the old man.

14. In which paragraph did you realize who the young man and the old man are?

15. What would be the best title for this story? Write your answer on the blank line at the beginning of the story.

 a. North Wind and Spring Defeat Winter
 b. Spring and Fawn Defeat Winter
 c. Winter and Fawn Defeat Spring

16. The story talks about
 a. seasons
 b. generations
 c. both a. and b.

B. Go back to the story in Activity A and find all the italicized words. Then draw arrows from the italicized words to the words they refer to.

C. From the context of the story guess the meaning of the italicized words and write a synonym for each word on the blank lines.

1. When the world was new, an old man was *wandering* around.

   _____

2. Leaves *shriveled* and fell from the trees.

   _____

Weather and Climate · 171

3. "No one can enter my *lodge*," said the old man.

4. The fire gave off a *flickering* light.

5. The North Wind went away, but the old man did not *stir*.

6. Someone was *striking* against the ice, so that pieces fell off.

7. When the young man *stirred* the fire it began to grow warm.

8. With his *chilly* breath the old man can freeze things.

9. Wherever Old Man Winter steps, the ground turns into *flint*.

10. Wherever Young Man Spring steps, the grasses *sprout* and snow melts away.

D. Read the three poems and decide which season each poem is talking about. Write the season on the blank line in the title. Then explain where in the poem you got the information.

1.

Waking

Can this be day?
It looks like night,
So thin and sulky
is the light.

A lonely sweeper
in the street
disturbs the dust
of last night's feet

And curtains open
splinter wide
give little sign
of life inside.

A stubborn car
with cough and wheeze
resents the turning
of the keys

While clockwork birds
sing "tin, tin, tin,"
to woo the weary
morning in;

And singing, singing
in my head,
How safe it was,
how warm,
in bed.

Irene Rawnsley

From *House of a Hundred Cats* by Irene Rawnsley, published by Metheun Children's Books. Reprinted by permission of Reed Consumer Books Ltd.

2.

Bee! I'm Expecting You!

Bee! I'm expecting you!
Was saying Yesterday
To Somebody you know
That you were due –

The Frogs got Home last Week –
Are settled, and at work –
Birds, mostly back –
The Clover warm and thick –

You'll get my Letter by
The seventeenth; Reply
Or better, be with me –
Yours, Fly.

Emily Dickinson

"Bee! I'm Expecting You!" reprinted by permission of the publishers and the Trustees of Amherst College from *The Poems of Emily Dickinson*, Thomas H. Johnson, ed., Cambridge, Mass.: The Belknap Press of Harvard University Press, Copyright © 1951, 1955, 1979, 1983 by the President and Fellows of Harvard College.

3.

About Caterpillars

What about caterpillars?
Where do they crawl
when the stars say, "Frost,"
and the leaves say, "Fall?"

Some go to sleep
in a white silk case when the winds say, "Blow!"
and the clouds say, "Race!"

Some sleep in bags
of woven brown
or curl in a ball
when the year says, "Frown."

None has the least little urge to know
what the world is like
when the sky says, "Snow."

Aileen Fisher

E. Match the season to the month by writing the letter of the appropriate month next to each season. What would your answer for the Northern Hemisphere look like and what would your answer for the Southern Hemisphere look like?

1. summer   a. October
2. fall   b. April
3. winter   c. December
4. spring   d. July

F. Look at the chart that describes the seasons in the imaginary country of Tikhan, located in the Southern Hemisphere. Write statements about the weather in this country using the information and whenever possible using the appropriate adverb of frequency (see the language box on p. 175).

Example:

In Tikhan, it *often* rains in the summer.

	Jan.	Feb.	March	April	May	June	July	Aug.	Sept.	Oct.	Nov.	Dec.
Precipitation (mm)	80*	80*	68**	34	15	2****	0	0	11	10	10**	40*
Temperature (°C)	40**	45**	35	25	10	1	5	3	18	19	21	35
Hours of Sunshine per Day	14	16	12	12	12	6	8	5	8	8	8	24

*Daily showers.
**Weekly storms.
***Hardly a change between day and night.
****Occasional light snowfall.

Adverbs of Frequency

When you write about the weather, you may need some special words to describe how often something happens. *Adverbs of frequency* tell your audience how often something occurs, for example, how often it rains or snows in your country. The following scale will help you to organize your presentation, so that your audience gets the correct ideas about the weather in your country.

In India it always rains in the summer.
Indonesia never has snow.

0	10	30	50	70	90	100% of the time
never	seldom rarely hardly ever	sometimes occasionally	often frequently	generally usually		always

G. Write about the seasons where you live or in a place you enjoyed visiting. Choose either task 1 or task 2.

1. If you want to write a report, you should try to answer the following questions.

   a. Is the place in the Northern or the Southern Hemisphere; is it close or far from the equator?
   b. How many seasons are there?
   c. What are the names of the seasons?
   d. How is the weather in each season?

2. If you want to write a poem about the weather in this city or country, try to write about the following ideas.

   a. What is the best season of the year? Why?
   b. How do you feel during the season you are writing about?
   c. Are there special things in nature that you like about this season?

176 · **Earthbound**

III. Living with the Climate

A. Look at the following headline from a newspaper. What weather condition is being discussed? What effect did this weather condition have?

> IN CHICAGO, WEEK OF HEAT LEAVES OVERFLOWING MORGUE

B. Brainstorm other effects that different kinds of weather can have on people's lives.

C. Look at the following headlines and answer the questions.

1. What weather condition is described in each headline?
2. What effect does the headline say the weather had? Can you explain further what might happen as a result of the bad weather?

> A WINTER OF DISASTER LEAVES THE BILLS TO PROVE IT

> GEORGIA FLOOD DEATH TOLL AT 19

> THANK LAST WEEK'S FREEZE FOR THIS WEEK'S SLICK ROADS

> AS WEATHER THAWS, TROUBLE WITH YOUTH STARTS TO HEAT UP

> *Hurricane Opal calms, leaving death and destruction*

D. The following pictures show three different places with very different weather conditions. Look at the pictures and describe all the things you can identify. Where do you think each picture was taken? How did you get to your conclusion?

a

b

c

E. Discuss or write about how the weather in these pictures affects the lifestyle in these places. For example, do people live in these places? What activities do these people have? How do the people make their livings?

Appendixes

Appendix A: Pronunciation Chart

Consonants

Symbol	Key Word
b	**b**ack
d	**d**ay
ð	**th**en
dʒ	**j**ump
f	**f**ew
g	**g**ay
h	**h**ot
j	**y**et
k	**k**ey
l	**l**ed
m	su**m**
n	su**n**
ŋ	su**ng**
p	**p**en
r	**r**ed
s	**s**oon
ʃ	fi**sh**ing
t	**t**ea
tʃ	**ch**eer
θ	**th**ing
v	**v**iew
w	**w**et
z	**z**ero
ʒ	plea**s**ure

Vowels

Symbol	Key Word
æ	b**a**d
ɑ	*AmE* f**ar**m
ɑː	c**a**lm
ɒ	*BrE* p**o**t
aɪ	b**i**te
aʊ	n**ow**
aɪə	t**ire**
aʊə	t**ower**
ɔ	*AmE* f**or**m
ɔː	c**augh**t
ɔɪ	b**oy**
ɔɪə	empl**oyer**
e	b**e**d
eə	th**ere**
eɪ	m**a**ke
eɪə	pl**ayer**
ə	**a**bout
əʊ	n**o**te
əʊə	l**ower**
ɜ	*AmE* b**ir**d

Symbol	Key Word
ɜː	b**ir**d
i	prett**y**
iː	sh**ee**p
ɪ	sh**i**p
ɪə	h**ere**
o	*AmE* p**or**t
uː	b**oo**t
ʊ	p**u**t
ʊə	p**oor**
ʌ	c**u**t

Appendix B: Units and Conversions

Length

U.S. Unit	U.S. Equivalents	Metric Equivalents
inch	—	2.54 centimeters
foot	12 inches	0.3048 meter
yard	3 feet, or 36 inches	0.9144 meter
mile	5,280 feet	1.61 kilometers

Area

U.S. Unit	U.S. Equivalents	Metric Equivalents
square mile	640 acres	2,590 square kilometers

Volume or Capacity

U.S. Unit	U.S. Equivalents	Metric Equivalents
pint	16 ounces	0.473 liter
quart	2 pints	0.946 liter
gallon	4 quarts	3.785 liters

Weight

U.S. Unit	U.S. Equivalents	Metric Equivalents
pound	16 ounces	453.59237 grams
ton	2,000 pounds	0.907 metric ton

Temperature

Fahrenheit (F)	Celsius (C)	Formula to Convert F into C
32°	0°	Degree C corresponds to (X°F − 32°F) divided by 1.8
212°	100°	

Appendix C: Directory of Environmental Organizations

Acid Rain Foundation, Inc.
1410 Varsity Drive
Raleigh, North Carolina 27606

Alliance to Save Energy
1725 K Street, NW #914
Washington, DC 20006

Center for Action on Endangered
  Species
175 West Main Street
Ayer, Massachusetts 01432

Center for Environmental Information
99 Court Street
Rochester, New York 14604

Clear Water Action
317 Pennsylvania Ave., SE
Washington, DC 20003

Earth Birthday Project
183 Pinehurst, #34
New York, New York 10033

Earthcare Network
330 Pennsylvania Ave., S.E.
Washington, DC 20037

Environmental Action Coalition
625 Broadway, 2nd Floor
New York, New York 10012

Environmental Defense Fund
257 Park Ave., South
New York, New York 10010

Friends of the Earth
218 D Street, SE
Washington, DC 20003

Global Tomorrow Coalition
1325 G Street, NW, Suite 915
Washington, DC 20005-3104

Greenpeace
1611 Connecticut Ave., NW
Washington, DC 20009

Greenpeace Action
1436 U Street, NW
Washington, DC 20009

The Institute for Earth Education
PO Box 288
Warrenville, Illinois 60555

Institute for Environmental
  Education
32000 Chagrin Boulevard
Cleveland, Ohio 44124

International Ecology Society
1471 Barclay Street
St. Paul, Minnesota 55106

National Geographic Society
1145 17th Street, NW
Washington, DC 20036

National Resources Defense Council
40 West 20th Street
New York, New York 10011

Rain Forest Alliance
295 Madison Ave., Suite 1804
New York, New York 10017

Soil and Water Conservation Society
7515 NE Ankeny Road
Ankeny, Iowa 50021

Solar Energy Research Institute
1617 Cole Blvd.
Golden, Colorado 80401

World Federalist Association
United Nations Office
777 United Nations Plaza
New York, New York 10017

World Resources Institute
1709 New York Ave., NW
Washington, DC 20006

World-Wide Fund for Nature
60 St. Clair Ave., E, Suite 201
Toronto, Ontario M4T 1N5

World Wildlife Fund
1250 24th Street, NW
Washington, DC 20037

Worldwatch Institute
1776 Massachusetts Ave., NW
Washington, DC 20036

World-Wide Fund for Nature
60 St. Clair Ave., E, Suite 201
Toronto, Ontario M4T 1N5

Appendix D: Glossary

Acid rain precipitation that is unusually acidic; it is the result of pollution that leads to a chemical reaction in the water vapor

Agriculture the science and practice of farming

Ash very small volcanic particles that are thrown out from a volcano

Atmosphere the layer of air that surrounds the earth (about 310 miles thick)

Basin large depression in the surface of the earth

Bay a part of a body of water that is surrounded by land

Boundary a line separating one political unit from another

Canyon a very deep and narrow valley

Climate a summary of weather conditions in a place or region over a period of time

Coal rocklike deposit that is rich in carbon and is used as a fuel

Condensation the change from a gas to a liquid

Core the center and hottest part of the earth, composed mainly of liquid metals

Crust the outermost layer of the earth, composed mainly of rocks

Dam a construction to stop the flow of water and regulate floods

Delta a fan-shaped area of land at the mouth of a river

Disaster a severe event that changes the landscape or disrupts the normal lives of people

Divide a mountain range that separates river systems

Dormant A volcano that has not erupted for many years is called dormant.

Dust fine powderlike particles

Earthquake a violent shaking of the earth's surface due to movements of crustal plates

Environment surroundings

Epicenter point on the earth's surface that is above the center of an earthquake

Equator an imaginary east-west line that goes around the globe halfway between the North and the South Poles

Erosion water or wind wash away soil

Eruption a sudden explosion

Evaporation liquid turns into gas

Extinction disappearance of a whole species of animals or plants

Fault the break in a body of rock

Flood unusually high flow of water in a river causing the water to cover surrounding area that is normally dry

Fog a condition in which the air near the surface of the earth contains a lot of water

Fold bend in the beds of rock

Fracture a clear break in a rock or mineral

Geyser a natural fountain of hot water

Glacier a large mass of moving ice

Gondwanaland a big continent that existed in the Southern Hemisphere before it broke into different continents (e.g., South America, Africa, India, Australia)

Greenhouse effect process in which the lower atmosphere and the earth's surface warm up

Grid system imaginary lines of latitude and longitude that are used to find places on a map

Groundwater water beneath the earth's surface

Hail little balls that fall from the clouds as rain

Hazardous waste any waste material that could be harmful for humans or for the environment

Hurricane a violent tropical storm

Hydroelectric power electrical energy that is created from moving water

International date line by international agreement the line where each new day begins (it follows the 180th meridian)

Irrigation bring water to farmland where there is not enough rainfall

Isthmus a narrow strip of land that connects two pieces of land

Lake an inland body of freshwater

Landslide a slide of loose rock and soil down a steep slope

Latitude the distance north or south of the equator, measured in degrees, minutes, and seconds

Laurasia a supercontinent that existed in the Northern Hemisphere before it separated into Asia, Europe, and North America

Lava molten rock on the surface of the earth (usually orange, red, or yellow in color and with a temperature of over 1,470°F)

Longitude the distance of a location, measured in degrees, minutes, and seconds, east or west of the prime meridian

Mantle the middle layer of the earth, composed mainly of very hot rock

Mercali scale uses numbers from 1–12 to measure the intensity of an earthquake by looking at the observable effects

Mid-Atlantic Ridge the mountain chain in the middle of the Atlantic Ocean floor

Monsoon a seasonal change in wind direction that often brings a change in weather (e.g., India gets the rainy season)

Mountain range a chain of mountains

Ozone layer the part of the atmosphere at a height of 10–20 miles where the form of oxygen called ozone occurs in higher concentration than usual; it absorbs harmful UV radiation before it gets to the ground

Pangaea the single continent from which all the current continents evolved

Appendix D · 189

Parallel an east-west line of latitude indicating distance north or south of the equator

Peak the top of a high mountain, or mountain in general

Pesticide a substance that kills pests such as bugs

Plate a piece of the earth's crust

Plate tectonics theory

Runoff water that flows off land into streams and other waterways

Scale the relation between the size of an area on a map and the actual size of that area on Earth

Sea a large body of saltwater

Seashore the land around a sea

Seismometer a device for measuring earthquake vibrations in the earth